Life

Happens

Rick Watson

10/12

Enjoy the Ride

Published by HomeFolk Media
Empire, Alabama
www.homefolkmedia.com
www.slosshollerscholar.com

Acknowledgement

When it comes to acknowledging the people who've helped me get to where I am today, I always fret that I'll leave someone out, because in the scheme of things, almost everyone you encounter throughout your life leaves a footprint on your psyche.

Even people you don't like and the ones who've treated you badly provide inspiration and motivation, if only to show the fatherless mongrels what you're made of.

Obviously, some leave much deeper footprints. I acknowledged several in my first book, but I'd be remiss if I didn't thank my friend and mentor Dale Short who edited *Life Happens*.

Thanks also to my friend Asa Faith Randolph, who gave the book a final going over.

And thanks to my wife Jilda who has stood beside me when a lesser woman would have bolted for a higher income tax bracket.

But I'd also like to thank our friends who've always been there to encourage, support, and kick my rear end when I needed it.

I hope you enjoy *Life Happens*.

Life

Happens

Contents

O•N•E

A Family of Restless Spirits

This week I've spent time at Davis Cemetery, where my folks are buried. Decoration is the second Sunday in June, and it takes a while to get the old cemetery in shape.

It's a peaceful place most of the time. My mom, dad and brothers are buried at the top of the hill, close to the service road that encircles the graveyard. I was there one evening this week, sitting on the tailgate of my truck, giving them updates about what's happening in my life.

I sat there for a while in silence, listening to the pines whispering to the wind and the sound of birds getting ready to turn in for the evening.

Off in the distance, I heard a freight train blowing as it approached Burnwell and Bergen, warning drivers to approach the crossings with care.

The sound of trains moving eastward and westward makes this a perfect place for my dad and my brothers, all of whom had an undercurrent of restlessness coursing through their souls.

In our younger days, whenever I went anywhere with my older brother Neil, he always walked quickly, like he had an appointment with destiny and he was running late.

When he graduated from high school, he moved up north for a time, to put some distance between himself and the hills and the hollows of Walker County.

He later moved to California to see if he could find what he was looking for out there but ended up moving back here, where he married and raised a family. He seemed happy and he loved his kids, but he died young at age 50, and I'm not sure if he ever found what he was looking for.

My younger brother Darren seemed even more restless than Neil. He left home soon after high school and moved to Birmingham, Atlanta, and later to Houston, Texas. He also died too young at the age of 33.

My dad seemed more restless than either of my brothers. He spent very little time at home. On weekends he'd be on the Warrior River, or he'd be driving around Walker County in his pickup, visiting with his old friends.

It was hard for him to sit still for any length of time. He always seemed to be searching, though he never said why.

Even though this next part happened more than 55 years ago, I remember it as if it were yesterday.

It was late one evening after the sun had slipped below the horizon to the west. We'd finished supper and he went out to the front porch to sip the last of his ice tea and smoke a coffin-nail, as he called it.

As he sat, the chains of the old wooden swing creaked and groaned. I crawled up into his lap to watch the lightning bug show that had just gotten underway. Off in the distance we heard the sound of an old freight train blowing for the crossing at Dora, and it chugged down a notch to change gears, but to me it sounded like it was taking a breath.

He said "Joe Ab," (don't ask me why he called me that) "I'm gonna ride that train one of these days."

I was too young then to realize how deep that seam of restlessness ran through his soul, but looking back, I get a sense of just how much he longed to be somewhere else at times.

Neither Dad nor my brothers ever had an opportunity to travel very much in their lifetimes. My prayer, as I sat on the tailgate of my pickup, was that they are now wandering the universe like hobos.

T·W·O

A Matter Of Time

I bought an hourglass several years ago and I keep it on my desk to make me mindful of time. I often tilt it over while I'm thinking, to watch the sand pour through. This morning as I watch the trickling sand, I'm reminded once again how brief our vacation on earth really is, and that life is truly a matter of time.

I read a book once called "Your Money or Your Life" that pointed out just how finite time is. The average man in America can expect to live to be about 75 ½, which is around 661,380 hours.

The average female normally lives an additional 43,800 hours. The idea behind the book is, how many hours of your life are you giving up to buy "stuff"? Cars, jewelry, shoes, and big houses? When I did the math, the numbers were sobering.

Everyone has to earn a living, unless you are born into money. But some folks live beyond their means, and spend too much of their lives trying to keep their heads above water.

It's a fact that "stuff" doesn't make you happy. Spending time with the people you love, or doing things that make you stronger, smarter, and better, do tend to make you happier.

My mama and daddy spent a chunk of time with us kids. When we were in school, Mama would set up the ironing board in the kitchen and iron clothes while watching us do our homework. She could spot-check our work and never miss a wrinkle.

I think they went to every Christmas play, little league game, or fall festival we were in.

They understood that it was only a matter of time before we grew up and left the nest for a life of our own.

Likewise, my grandparents -- who lived next door for much of my life -- invested a great deal of time in us kids. If I asked one question, I asked a million. I don't think it ever occurred to them to say, "Not now, son. I'm busy and don't have the time."

Do you ever wonder why some people are successful at running businesses, raising families, and at life in general? Or why some people are phenomenal guitar players, dancers, preachers, teachers, or athletes? There is usually talent involved with each of these callings, but perhaps the biggest factor is time.

Successful people devote the time to attain the life

they desire. Musicians spend countless hours of practice, doing mundane scales, riffs, and study, before becoming accomplished performers. The difference between mediocrity and brilliance is measured by the hands of time.

So many people spend valuable time on unimportant things. Once those grains of sand pass through the hourglass, you can never get them back.

A very good friend of mine, who had a run-in with cancer a few years ago, told me that she no longer spends time with people she doesn't like.

During her professional career, she attended functions and gatherings with people she didn't know. After a short time, she realized she didn't want to know them. "It's not that they were bad people," she explained. "They just wanted different things from life. I made a decision to spend the time I have left with people I enjoy being around."

These days she spends quality time tending her garden and her animals. She visits with her friends. She reads. She drinks green tea in the afternoon while watching yellow and purple finches on the feeders in her yard. The time she spends in stillness seems to make her stronger.

I thought about my friend as I watched the sand slipping through the hourglass today and I understand her appreciation for every passing moment.

T·H·R·E·E

Age

My late octogenarian mother-in-law Ruby Phillips said the only time she felt old was when she looked in the mirror.

I'm kind of like Ruby, in that I don't feel that old. Well, maybe sometimes when I roll out of bed and my knees squeak like the door hinges of an old VW Bug.

But recently the age thing slapped me in the face like a jilted debutant. Jilda and I attended a writer's event and got a room at a nice hotel near the conference.

We hauled more stuff up there than we normally do. We took guitars, a camera bag, the laptop, and a box of books for me to hawk at the conference. This was in addition to our luggage and Jilda's makeup bag.

A bellhop promptly loaded all our stuff and headed toward the room. I was checking e-mail on my phone, so Jilda and the bellhop were a few steps ahead. I heard him say, "I see you brought your dad with you." That would have been OK with me if he'd been trying to score some points with Jilda, but he was serious.

Jilda smiled as she looked back over her shoulder at me. When the bellhop looked back at me, I blazed him with a look that probably would have caused second degree burns on his face and neck had he been a step closer.

Once he unloaded the bags he lingered for a tip. I thought to myself, we'll find cures for cancer, heart disease, and stupidity before I give you a tip, sonny boy. Of course he probably could have taken early retirement with the tip Jilda gave him.

When the door closed, she didn't say a word, but simply smiled and began unpacking her bags. I found myself in a snit.

I shouldn't have been surprised. She's always looked young for her age. Whenever we went to places that had age requirements, they checked her ID -- until she was over thirty.

Once when we went to the state fair, there was an age-guesser guy there. He was about to guess Jilda's age when I walked up. He looked at me, then looked at her, and after sizing me up, he guessed her age right on the money. He told her before she walked away that it was looking at me that gave him a clue as to her age. She was miffed at me for the rest of the evening.

I believe age has more to do with how you think, how you act, and how well you take care of your body, than the number of years you've lived here on earth.

I've met 20-year-olds that looked and acted like they were older than fossils. Conversely, I've met people in their 90s who radiated energy and vitality. As a result, they looked much younger than their years. These people tend to expect the best out of life, and they usually get it.

I interviewed a 90-year-old woman back in the spring and she still lived alone, had an active social life, and drove a convertible. When I asked her if there was a secret to aging gracefully, she smiled and said:

"Do things that excite you, learn to laugh, spend time outside, don't eat or drink too much, and take care of your knees, because you'll miss them when they're gone."

I could not agree more.

F·O·U·R

Appalachian-Americans

My good friend Steve sent me a note this morning with an update on political correctness. It seems that it's no longer appropriate for people above the Mason-Dixon line, and Yankees from other parts of the country, to call us folks from northern Alabama, north Georgia, Tennessee, North Carolina, South Carolina, Virginia or Kentucky by the derogatory term "hillbilly." From this day forward, we should be called Appalachian-Americans.

Dang, I'm glad somebody finally woke up and smelled the biscuits. Some folks feel that just because we're fond of fishin' with dynamite, makin' our own whiskey, and datin' our cousins, they can talk down to us by callin' us hillbillies.

Sure, a lot of us (including me) have a few cars up on blocks in our yards. But if they don't have motors they don't count, do they? And as the redneck joke goes, "If my back porch fell down, I might lose a dog or two." Does that give anyone the right to look down on us?

I don't know about you, but in my view, an occasional fist fight at a wedding or funeral adds interest to events and tends to make them more memorable. "Yeah, Sally came down with a hard right hook and broke old Ben's nose and then yanked a handful of his hair out. Too bad he wasn't alive to defend himself."

Sure, our murder rate might be a little out of whack. However, George Wallace explained this back in the Sixties when he was interviewed on 60 Minutes. When one of the commentators asked why our murder rate was so high in Alabama, Wallace quickly shot back, "I guess we just have more people that need killing." Now that puts the hay down to where the goats can get it!

I know that folks from the South see a few more UFOs than other places on the globe, but if I were an alien, I think I too would rather land in a place like Walker County where the women are pretty and folks talk slow enough to understand.

While establishing an intergalactic rapport, they could snack on some good old Southern fried chicken, cathead biscuits and sweet tea (which I don't believe exists anywhere in the universe, outside the south).

The thing is, I love hillbillies. I don't know of anyone who can watch an episode of "The Beverly Hillbillies" without smiling. If you can watch the "Dukes of Hazzard" and not see some kinfolks in there, you are simply not being truthful with yourself.

The fact is, the word hillbilly (or redneck for that matter) doesn't really bother me. Anyone could take one look at me, my kinfolks, and my friends and they'd probably say "yep, that's a bunch of hillbillies." But some of the kindest folks on the planet come from the hills and hollows of the south.

Also, statistics show that folks from the south donate more money to charity than any other place in the country.

Where else have you seen people who don't even know the deceased, pull to the side of the road out of respect while a funeral procession passes? In the past, when I've ridden in those funeral processions, this simple act of kindness always put a lump in my throat.

In the spirit of political correctness, the proper name for us may be Appalachian-Americans, but as far as I'm concerned, you can just call me a hillbilly.

F·I·V·E

Autumn

The Autumnal Equinox occurs this coming Tuesday at 4:18 a.m. I'm on vacation this week, so I plan to set my clock and get up just to make sure everything happens on time and without incident.

Yes, autumn is upon us, but it didn't take the Farmer's Almanac or a Wikipedia Internet search to tell me fall was around the corner because I could see it in the quality of the light filtering through the oak and pine trees. When ironwood leaves turn the color of home-churned butter and sumac leaves turn sunset red, you know that frost cannot be far behind.

People love fall of the year for many reasons and I could make a list a mile long. My list would start with autumn leaves. It's not only the color, which here in Alabama can be stunning, but also the smell of burning leaves. (They don't taste that good, but two out of three ain't bad.)

One of my chores when I was a kid was raking leaves from under the gigantic cottonwood and sycamore trees in our yard in Sloss. I would rake mountain-sized piles and then I'd leap in like a Hawaiian cliff diver.

I wasn't allowed to burn the leaves unless one of the older kids was around, but when I'd had as much fun as I could stand, my older brother Neil would fire up those piles of leaves. I sat on our concrete steps for hours and watched those burning leaves until there was nothing left but embers.

Even today, a hint of autumn smoke puts a smile on my face. In the blink of an eye, I'm 10 years old and sitting on those concrete steps again.

I also love the sky in autumn. It seems to be a richer shade of blue and I don't believe the moon gets any prettier than in the fall. Last year as we headed home after a visit with our nephew and his wife who live in Oakman, we saw a light filtering through the trees.

We weren't sure what it was at first, but when we came to a clearing we saw the full moon as bright as a spotlight just above the horizon.

Jilda and I got into a competition to come up with a word that best described the moon. "It's the color of orange sherbet," I suggested. That was close, but Jilda won the prize when she said, "It's a Dreamsicle Moon." I immediately conceded because I knew I would not come up with anything that rivaled that description.

Autumn, to me, is the best time of year to walk. We have a yard full of older dogs and there's nothing they love better than going for a walk. When the weather warms, they walk for a while but they soon get hot, seek the shade of the back porch, and wait for us to return. But in autumn, when the sun is warm and the air is crisp, they run around as if they were pups.

Another reason I love autumn is the harvest. Our apples turn a deep crimson a few weeks before the first frost, and are sweeter than dime-store candy.

The veggies that we grow and store in the summer are biding their time until the first cold snap. Jilda then builds the masterpiece that is her vegetable soup. I bake up a pone of my world-famous cornbread, and we get down to some serious eating.

Yes, I enjoy all seasons. But thanks to football, carving Halloween pumpkins, as well as the aroma and taste of Thanksgiving turkey, I think autumn just might be my favorite.

S·I·X

Beach

Most people prefer the beach in late spring or summer when the sun is hot and the ocean is warm as bath water. But Jilda and I love the beach in the fall and winter.

We drove down this past weekend and took the rain with us. The temperature was warm, so we opened the patio of the condo as we unpacked and listened to the pounding surf. Before dark, we stepped down to the water and leaned into a stiff wind coming off the gulf.

There was not another soul on the beach in either direction for as far as we could see.

As we stood there we could smell the rain mixed with the salty ocean air. When the first drops began to pepper our skin, we headed back to the condo and whipped up some hot tea.

We backed the patio chairs up close to the wall and sat for a while listening to the rain ticking on palm fronds out by the pool. It felt good to be alive.

Monday, I got up early to work on some stories I'd been

writing and I let Jilda sleep in. That's a luxury she rarely gets to enjoy.

At lunch, we drove from Orange Beach toward Gulf Shores looking for a good place to eat. We decided on a beachside cafe called Bahama Bob's.

By the time we were seated on the patio, the rain was coming down in sheets and the red surf-warning flags were blowing so hard it looked like they'd been starched and ironed.

We ordered oyster po'boys with home fries for lunch, and sweet tea. While waiting for our orders to arrive, we listened to the wind and rain play the metal roof like a steel drum.

I heard Jilda chuckling and when I looked to see what was causing the mirth, I saw a sign on the café wall that said, "All unattended children will be used as crab bait." I smiled too as I read the sign.

The main reason for our trip to the beach this time was that organizers for the Frank Brown International Songwriter's Festival invited us to perform at this year's festival.

Hundreds of songwriters and thousands of music lovers from all over the world converge each November on Orange Beach, and Gulf Shores, Alabama, as well as Pensacola, Florida to celebrate music and songwriters.

This was the 26th annual festival and we had the opportunity to play the Flora-Bama -- which is where the festival began.

The Flora-Bama is a bar that sits on Perdido Key in Pensacola, but its western wall is only six feet from the Alabama state line, thus the name Flora-Bama.

Hurricane Ivan scored a direct hit on the cultural landmark, but the owners cobbled it back together and it remains a popular area hot spot.

Playing on the stage of the Flora-Bama was on our Bucket List (the list of things we wanted to do before we die). We've been to the Flora-Bama in the past and sometimes the crowd can be quite rowdy.

The songs we write are definitely not loud, and they would never be considered dance music, so we weren't sure how we'd be received.

As it turns out, we held our own, and for the most part the audience listened while we sang our songs.

We didn't go on stage until after 10 p.m. so it was after midnight by the time we got back to the condo. Since Jilda had to work on Wednesday, we were up at the crack of dawn packing the car for the return trip home.

I stepped to the beach just before we left and, though the sun had not come up, the horizon to the east went from a thousand shades of orange to the deep indigo blue of the night sky. It looked like it would be another beautiful day.

As vacations go, it was short on time, but long on quality, and the memories we made are already golden.

S·E·V·E·N

Barefooted

When I was a kid growing up in Sloss Hollow, the bottoms of my feet were tougher than the soles of most store-bought shoes.

That's because from the middle of May to Labor Day, I never wore shoes unless I went to church or somewhere else shoes were required, which was rare.

Even when the days got hotter than the devil's welding torch, and the August sun baked tar bubbles from between the gravel on the paved road, I didn't wear shoes.

There were times I had to scrape tar off the bottoms of my feet with kerosene and a stick.

My feet could get really dirty during the day, but they had to be fairly clean before going to bed at night.

Trying to slip into the sack with dirty feet was useless because my mama had laser-scanning capabilities back then. She could be ironing a pair of dungarees in the kitchen and spot a dirty foot headed toward the bedroom, using only the dim light from our old Philco black-and-white TV set.

Mama had an old photograph in her picture box that was taken with her trusty Kodak camera. It was a picture of a bunch of kids in front of the house.

When you look closely at the picture, you can tell which kids were from up north visiting Alabama for the summer, because they all had on shoes.

The hillbilly kids would poke fun at their Yankee cousins until they shed their shoes and toughened up their feet.

By the time they went home at the end of summer, they had to be reminded to take their shoes with them.

The only tennis shoes I'd ever heard of were Keds and Converse All Stars, but I didn't own a pair until I went to high school and needed them for gym class.

A lot of folks said you can run faster and jump higher in tennis shoes, but I never bought into that malarkey. I felt like I could outrun the wind in my bare feet.

The beauty of being barefoot was that you didn't have to waste time sitting down and untying shoes when you came to a creek. If you were barefoot, you could walk right into the water without breaking stride. Bare feet felt like freedom to me.

Fast forward to now -- since I've been without

employment, I've spent a lot more time barefooted. It still feels great most of the time. But when I walk on anything other than grass, I do a little dance step that looks like a cross between a Native American rain dance and a drunk doing the "Monster Mash" that was so popular back in the day.

It seems like I'm more connected to the earth when I don't wear shoes.

Walking in a freshly plowed garden feels especially good to me. You can tell a great deal about the soil when you're barefooted. You can tell if the moisture content is right, you can tell if the soil has too much or too little clay, or if you need to run over the plot one more time with the tiller.

Of course, you can buy soil test kits that would probably be more accurate, but you'd lose that connection to the earth.

Some might say I'm a little too old to go shoeless and that I might look a little goofy when I walk on rough surfaces, but it's a small price to pay for that feeling of freedom.

E·I·G·H·T

BISCUIT

I am a biscuit connoisseur. The fact that I was born and raised in Sloss Holler, I think, qualifies me as an authority on biscuits.

I don't consider myself a biscuit snob though, because I like all kinds of biscuits. I automatically disqualify the ones that come in cans and the ones they eat with tea in England because they're really just cookies.

It's here in the good old South that we make real biscuits.

My mama used to make biscuits that were as crunchy as a scone, especially the bottoms.

There was an old green bowl she kept on the fridge that she used for biscuit making. She'd sift the flour with a hand-cranked sifter, toss in a little baking soda, a dash or two of salt, a "chunk" of lard, and a few cups of fresh buttermilk.

Then she'd slowly mix the concoction together. When the dough was like clay, she'd fold it over and over until it was just right.

With a rolling pin she'd roll the dough out on a sideboard and use a tea glass to punch out perfectly round biscuits. Next, she'd arrange them in an iron skillet "greased" with lard (of course), and pop them babies in the oven.

They came out of the oven golden brown all over. There was enough lard in those biscuits to make your heart flutter when the cholesterol hit your bloodstream.

In fact, most of my mama's recipes started off with, "Take a chunk of lard and add......"

Some folks bought lard in gallon buckets back then, but mama had her lard delivered in bulk by a truck once a month. Hogs feared her.

When I was drafted into the Army, my basic training was in Fort Campbell, Kentucky. That's far enough south that at least they knew what a biscuit was.

Unfortunately, the cooks hadn't perfected the art of biscuit making. When I pointed this out to the mess sergeant, he was not amused, so I found myself on KP (kitchen patrol) for three days.

My job was to peel mountains of potatoes and after lunch, to clean the cracks in the kitchen floor with a toothbrush. I learned to keep my culinary comments to myself.

When I got to Fort Monmouth, New Jersey, I had a feeling they were too far north of the Mason-Dixon Line to know about biscuits. This was confirmed when I asked for one that first day. The cook he looked at me as if I were speaking Swahili.

I'd learned my lesson in Kentucky and didn't dare bad-mouth the mess sergeant, so I moped off to my table and sulked as I munched on wilted toast.

When I got back home to mama's house from the Army, I was so anxious to have me some homemade biscuits that I felt like eating lard with a spoon straight from the bucket.

But mama got in the kitchen, fried up some eggs, made a pan of grits, fried some ham with red-eye gravy, and a huge pan of biscuits. I was back in heaven.

Jilda learned to make biscuits from her mom. Ruby's biscuits were not like my mom's, but were delightful nonetheless. They were like toasted clouds. Those biscuits were light, fluffy in the middle, and brown on the top and bottom.

Her family introduced me to many new ways of eating biscuits. Not only did they eat them with eggs, grits, and bacon, but they sometimes ate cheese inside theirs.

They'd munch them with sausage and a slice of tomato inside. Sometimes they'd break them in two, pour fresh honey or sorghum syrup all over, and eat them with a fork. I discovered that all of these were good ways to enjoy biscuits.

Jilda made biscuits this morning. Hers are a cross between the two kinds our mothers made.

She doesn't use lard, so my blood doesn't slow down to a trickle when I eat them, but they're scrumptious just the same. I would know. As I mentioned before, I am a connoisseur.

N·I·N·E

The Brain-Full Syndrome

As I read Dale Short's column this week in the *Daily Mountain Eagle*, I almost jumped off the couch and shouted "Hallelujah!" The column was about having the feeling that his brain was full. I can name that tune in one note.

I'm afflicted by the full-brain syndrome and it's never more evident than when I'm trying to come up with ideas for weekly columns.

My head is so full of trivia, technical garbage, and other bits of useless knowledge that navigating around inside there trying to find something fresh to write about is like swimming in a vat of cold grits.

I must have realized this sometime back because I've been unconsciously employing some safeguards to keep my head from bursting open like a ripe melon.

For example, I have a pass-through filter that I often use when Jilda is talking to me. I can sit there and look deeply engrossed in the conversation but in reality she might as well be talking to a stump. The details slide right through my brain as if my ear canals were sprayed with WD-40.

She could have explained in minute detail what she's planning to cook that night, and a few minutes later I'll ask, "What's for supper?"

She rolls her eyes and gives me the *Reader's Digest* version of what we're having. Then when we sit down to eat, I'll say, "Wow, we're having roast chicken! I was hoping we'd have that."

It's at these times she utilizes what I call her "laser stare." That's the look that wordlessly says, "I have friends who would help me put you down, chop your body in little pieces, and put you in the deep freezer."

I tend to get a little antsy here because I know it's true. I love her friends, but if it came down to choosing between Jilda and me, they'd bring freezer bags and gas for the chainsaw.

Another brain-space saving technique I use is electronic reminders. I have all kinds of devices that beep, chirp, ring, buzz, vibrate, and otherwise notify me.

When I have something really important to remember, I'll set up reminders on all the devices. When the appointed time comes, it sounds like noon at a grandfather-clock repair shop.

I think part of the cause of the full-brain syndrome is

the velocity of information that comes at us daily.

Back in the day, you got information via the "brogan net". That's when a neighbor (usually wearing brogans) walked over to your house in the evenings, sat out on the porch, and chewed the fat. They'd discuss local gossip and other news.

They usually headed home before the "skeeters" got too bad. Mama would often send them on their way with a few fresh tomatoes, a basket of peas, or a jar of chow-chow.

These days, not only do we have newspapers, TV, and radio all vying for brain time, but also computers and smart phones streaming news, sports and weather 24x7.

Whose brain would not get full after a while? After reading Dale's column, I realize that I am not alone. And that makes me feel better.

T·E·N

Ol' Buddy And The Bank

We have a little mutt we call Ol' Buddy. We inherited him from Jilda's mom, Ruby, when she passed away. Ruby actually called him Baby, but there's no way I would have a dog named Baby.

I was convinced that the name Baby would cause unresolved issues with his self-image, so I promptly changed his name to Ol' Buddy. The name seemed to fit him much better, and he didn't whine as much.

I've written about Buddy in the past. In fact, the story I wrote about how we first got him is a story that many readers remember most. Folks do love their dogs.

The little mutt makes friends wherever he goes. He loves everybody, except small children. I'm not sure if he views them as competition or "other," but I have to keep my best eye on him when our young nieces and nephews are around.

At our local bank, Ol' Buddy is like a rock star. When we turn into the drive-through to make a deposit, he gets beside himself. He starts barking and wagging his tail, as he ricochets off the arm rests. By the time it's our turn at the window, he's in our lap trying his best to get to the retractable cash drawer.

Banking at our branch comes to a standstill as the tellers come over to the window to howdy up with Ol' Buddy.

By this time, the dog is putting on a show. When the tellers say something to him through the tinny speakers, he cocks his head like the RCA Victor dog. We have to restrain him to keep him from licking the teller window and hopping into the money tray for a ride inside. Heaven forbid that should happen, because we'd never get him out.

When they complete our transaction and send the cash drawer back out to us, there's always a doggy treat in it. To Ol' Buddy, that's commerce at its best.

Recently, Jilda ran by the (different) bank that handles our business account. As she approached the window, Ol' Buddy got excited. But when they arrived, much to his dismay, there was no excitement from inside the bank. Everything seemed to continue as usual. To a small creature who views himself as the center of the universe, this was unthinkable.

I'm guessing the main thought running through his mind was "Money changers! I have a lot of clout with my daddy, Ms. MoneyGirl, and when I get home you'll be in big trouble!"

To complete the slight, when the money drawer came back out the only thing it contained was a receipt, which he promptly chewed up and left in a damp clump on the floorboard.

I guess I need to have a talk with the banking team because there's one thing they need to understand--when Ol' Buddy ain't happy, I ain't happy. All that Ol' Buddy wants is a little R-E-S-P-E-C-T.

Dog biscuits don't hurt, either.

E·L·E·V·E·N

The Old Carwash

Many times when I need inspiration for a column, I flip through old photographs. When I came across the picture of me doing my Charles Atlas imitation in front of our old Ford Fairlane, a story came to mind that I thought I would share.

When I was growing up in Sloss, there was a shallow place in Horse Creek where people would go to wash their cars. I'm not sure where the creek originates, but it meanders through east Walker County and is fed by pure icy water from somewhere deep in the earth.

Oftentimes on warm Saturday and Sunday afternoons, there would be a line of folks waiting their turn to wash the coal dust and road grime off their old cars.

It was usually a family affair. The dad would drive the car into the creek, shut off the engine, and then a herd of kids would bail out with buckets and rags and commence handwashing their car.

After soaping up the car, everyone would take their bucket, scoop it full of water from the creek, and start flinging it on the car to rinse off the soap.

It was not uncommon for this segment of the cleanup detail to get out of hand. Someone would intentionally take a bad aim and all of a sudden, little sister had a face full of water. All such attacks required full and immediate retaliation. Before long, the washers were wetter than the car.

One Saturday in August when I was about 10 years old, we headed out to wash the Ford.

I was soaked to the bone and I'd had about as much fun as I could stand in the creek, so I wandered off downstream to check out the scenery. I was as barefooted as the day I was born.

I came to an old hickory log that had fallen next to the creek and was about to step over.

Just before I put my foot down I glanced at the ground and what I saw put "the fear" in me. Lying in a sunny spot next to the log was a Cottonmouth Moccasin that looked to be as big as my leg.

Somehow, I managed an evasive maneuver that was a cross between a high jump and a double-back flip.

I let out a blood-curdling scream that made my entire family unit come running at full speed.

My brother Neil must have had a similar experience in

the past, because he grabbed the .22 rifle out of the truck before he ran down the creek.

The Cottonmouth didn't flee like a regular snake. He took stock of the gathering crowd trying to decide if he could take us all on.

Just as Neil arrived, the evil beast slowly slid into the creek and began to swim downstream.

Neil was excited as he shouldered the rifle and then he fired off about eight rounds, none of which came anywhere near the snake. The last we saw of the tubular Satan, he was swimming downstream at a leisurely pace.

The story became part of our family's lore. By the time we got home to tell mama, the snake had doubled in size and looked as if it had eaten a small child before I came upon it.

We continued going to the Horse Creek carwash for years, but to this day, I never go barefoot on a creek bank and I always look twice before stepping over a log.

T·W·E·L·V·E

Charlie

We have an old shaggy dog named Charlie. On most days he looks like he just got out of the spin cycle of our Maytag washing machine, and at other times like Albert Einstein on a bad hair day. Like most of our mutts, Charlie is a "throwaway" dog.

We live on a dead-end road where some people think it's acceptable to dump their garbage, deer carcasses, and unwanted animals for us to enjoy. But Charlie's story is a little different.

Charlie lived with a family across the road from our house. They had three or four young children, along with Charlie and another dog of questionable pedigree.

The family lived there about a year but they kept to themselves. On warm days you could hear the kids out in the yard playing. I've often heard one of the little girls calling Charlie up for supper. "CHOL-LEEE, come here boy, CHOL-LEEE!" she'd call. You could see her and the unkempt mutt rolling around in the grass having a large time.

I think the father must have lost his job and gotten

behind on the rent, because one day they were gone with no forwarding address. The only things they left behind were their two dogs.

The mobile home is a rental and there have been a number of families who lived there through the years, so it was not an unusual situation. Except, they'd left Charlie and his friend.

We assumed they'd be back, and apparently Charlie and his friend did too because they camped out at the end of the driveway and spent their time looking down the road, waiting for their family to return. But they never did.

It was hard for Jilda and me to imagine the family abandoning the dogs, knowing how much their children loved the critters. While it is true that dogs are a man's best friend, the opposite is not always true.

After a few days, Jilda started leaving bowls of food and water for the dogs up in their driveway. I didn't realize this at first, though I would not have objected. We already had four dogs of our own, so I thought about taking them to the Humane Society where they could hopefully find a home.

But Jilda pointed out that the two dogs seemed to be soulmates and that the chances of someone taking two adult, scruffy-looking mutts were slim.

After several weeks, Charlie and his friend Dawg began to venture into our yard and eventually they decided to live with us.

A few years ago, Dawg went to that happy fire hydrant in the sky and Charlie mourned the loss for months. He can be quite moody at times.

Charlie (who is older than Dick Clark) is the smartest dog at our house. We learned the hard way that he had figured out how to open the gates of our backyard chain-link fence. We came home from an overnight trip and all our dogs (except Charlie) greeted us from the front yard which is outside the fence. I assumed a prowler had been in our back yard and left the gates open, but nothing had been disturbed.

A few days later, Jilda watched out the back door as Charlie leaned up on the back gate and knocked the latch open with his nose. Our other dogs darted out the gate to freedom while Charlie ambled back to the deck.

As Jilda stepped outside, Charlie looked up as if to say, "Those dogs are not smart, and you should put them down as soon as possible". I'm convinced that if the dog had thumbs, he'd be able to crack safes.

Charlie is part of our family and we love this wacky mutt. He loves it here too, but sometimes on warm, sunny days, he seems to get a little melancholy, and he will amble up to the end of our driveway and look off down the road.

T·H·I·R·T·E·E·N

Driving School

I'd never heard of a driver's safety course and I probably would have considered it a waste of time when I was younger, until I got an up-close and personal demonstration of its merits.

My cousin Randall's family moved off up north when I was very young and they moved back home to Alabama when I was about 16. He'd gone to junior high school in Indiana and one of the requirements there was driving school.

He was an excellent driver. He honored all traffic signs, used his blinkers when making turns, and always tested his brakes prior to needing them at stop signs or unexpected animal events (deer darts and dog dares).

His cousins tended to have fun at his expense because as all Southerners know, speed limits and traffic signs are simply suggestions for the uninitiated. Most of us thought (and apparently still think) that turn signals are optional and used mainly by old geezers with faint hearts.

One spring morning as I rode with Randall in his newly purchased (old) Renault, I realized the value of driving school.

I should have been leery of the Renault from the start, as it was one of those small cars that resemble a roller skate with windshield wipers. Of all places, the contraption was built in France.

Randall got a good deal on the Renault and had it serviced by a local mechanic. The mechanic had never seen a Renault before, but used this repair job as an excuse to buy a new set of metric wrenches.

When we picked the car up, it seemed to be doing fine. For some reason that I don't recall, we headed through Kershaw Hollow and across Fire Tower Mountain. Now, Fire Tower isn't really a mountain in the sense that most Westerners know, but for us hillbillies here in these parts it's about as high as it gets. That's the reason the forestry service built a fire tower up there.

As we crested the hill, Randall tested the brakes just as his training had taught him. When he pressed the brake, it went all the way down. I could hear metal against metal as the pedal banged repeatedly against the floorboard.

I've driven old cars all my life and I knew that sound because I'd heard it many times before when my jalopies got too low on brake fluid.

My cousin never panicked. He simply reached between the seat for the emergency brake, which he expertly ripped up to stop the runaway skateboard with doors.

I'm not sure what happened, but not only did the car NOT stop, it picked up speed. The road seemed to drop off before us like a cliff. Randall, still focused on maintaining control, said "Hold on."

Now, that's an instruction he really didn't have to give. I don't think he'd ever been down Fire Tower Mountain before, but I had. I knew it was a good mile and a half of steady descent with hairpin turns. With uncanny presence, he whipped the steering wheel this way and that and continued trying to shift down into a lower gear to slow the car down.

The ride down that mountain was like a roller-coaster. Before we got to the bottom, I'd said the world's longest prayer, confessed all my sins, and said goodbye to mama.

It's a miracle that we made it to the bottom without flipping over one of the embankments, being thrown out, smacking our heads against oak trees, and being eaten by wild animals before our family and friends discovered our bones.

When I unfolded myself out of the Renault at the bottom, I noticed that there were dents in the roof where my hands had pushed to hold on. I'm guessing the seat covers had a hole made by my backside.

From that day forward, I never made fun of cousin

Randall for having gone to driving school. In fact, I think it saved our lives.

F·O·U·R·T·E·E·N

Embarrassed

Life is a very good teacher. I've talked about the lessons I've learned in past columns, but it seems we're never too old to learn – especially me.

Let me start at the beginning. When I first started writing a weekly column in the *Mountain Eagle*, people would come up to me on occasion to say they read my column. I've always been flattered by this gesture.

These days, as my work appears in more and more publications, it's become very common for people to approach Jilda and me when we're in restaurants and grocery stores to say that they read my work. Since I often talk about Jilda in my writings, people recognize her when we're out together.

Recently a woman said to Jilda, "It must be fun living with Rick!" I'm a little surprised that Jilda didn't roll her eyes, but she simply smiled and said, "He's a lot more amusing in print than he is at home."

Then a few weeks ago I ran down to Walmart to pick up a few things while Jilda was working.

As I walked around the store, I saw a couple from a distance looking in my direction and smiling. I thought to myself, these are people who recognized me from the paper.

I smiled, nodded my head in acknowledgement, and finished up with the shopping. The things I needed took me all over the store.

After I loaded my stuff in the truck and got in to drive away, I noticed my pants were unzipped.

I sat there for a long moment and then I remembered the couple on Aisle 12 smiling and looking at me.

In my mind, I was trying to figure out if they were smiling because they recognized me as the guy who writes for the paper, or were they smiling and saying to themselves: "Look at that guy prancing around Walmart with his pants unzipped!"

Or, worse yet: "Look, there's Rick Watson, the guy who writes for the paper, prancing around Walmart with his pants unzipped!"

For the record I was NOT prancing, but I think you get the picture. Even though I was sitting alone in my truck, my face started a slow blush that originated somewhere around my socks.

I debated on whether I should go back into Walmart and try to find the couple to apologize, but it occurred to me that the whole store could have seen me traipsing around.

If my first blush wasn't thorough enough, my brain threw up a fresh coat of crimson for good measure. When I looked in the mirror, it looked like I was sunburned.

When Jilda got home I told her the story and she laughed so hard she spewed ice tea on the coffee table. I have a feeling the next time one of those women makes a comment about how much fun it is living with me, she'll tell them this story.

Since this episode, I've been so paranoid that I'm tempted to wear only pants with elastic waistbands and no zippers.

I'm here to tell you that whenever you get too cocky, life will bring you down a peg or two. When it comes to zippers, I've learned my lesson.....ALWAYS CHECK THEM!

F·I·F·T·E·E·N

Every Day's a School Day

My wife Jilda and I wrote a song with our friend Tracy Reynolds called "Life 101." In the chorus it says "Sometimes you get the test, before you get the lesson". I was reminded this week just how true those words are.

I'm planning some foundation work on the barn and our old storage shed so I bought a spiffy new concrete mixer. On the way home from the tool store, I stopped by a local hardware store and bought four 80-pound bags of concrete to get started.

I almost busted a gut loading the bags and I knew I didn't want to lug each sack a few hundred feet to the shed, so I fetched the wheelbarrow for the job.

My old wheelbarrow has a flat tire, so I used the new garden tool which is a combination wheelbarrow and cart. It's ergonomically designed with two wheels in front and a handle that is a single bar across the back so that you can pull or push it. It's perfect for most small hauling jobs.

So anyway, I positioned the wheelbarrow/cart at the

back of the truck and I then hoisted the 80-pound bag of concrete off the back of the truck and dropped it into the wheelbarrow.

Now, I didn't take physics in school. But if I had, I would have understood things like gravity, force, balance, and Newton's Third Law of Motion which says, "To every action there is an equal and opposite reaction. The action and reaction act on two different bodies simultaneously."

Having missed those lessons was costly because as soon as I dropped those 80-pounds onto the front of that wheelbarrow, the front plunged downward, and the handle sprang up with remarkable speed and whacked me across the nose so hard that it made me see stars.

I decided to sit down right there in the driveway and think about life, liberty, and the pursuit of knowledge. It also gave me a moment to shake those stars out of my head.

I looked around to see if any of the neighbors saw the mishap. Doing something stupid is bad enough, but when someone sees you do something stupid, you not only have to deal with the mishap, you have to deal with the embarrassment too.

As it turns out, all I had to deal with was excruciating pain, bleeding nose, and the possibility of having two black eyes. The headache eventually subsided, so all in all, I think I was lucky. And I learned something valuable.

Someone could have told me a thousand times to be careful when loading heavy objects on wheelbarrows, and I probably would not have learned a thing. But getting decked by a wheelbarrow handle traveling at the speed of light brought the lesson home.

I can promise you this, I will, from this day forward, be very careful when loading heavy objects on ANYTHING!

The chorus to the song I mentioned above goes like this:

Every day is a school day
No matter how old you are
Sometimes the test comes before the lesson
Welcome to life 101.

S·I·X·T·E·E·N

Farming Is Not So Easy

I absolutely love gardening. The spring holds such promise of an abundant harvest. But this year instead of feeling like I have a green thumb, I feel more like Eddie Albert in the old TV comedy series "Green Acres."

In early spring our young peach tree had hundreds of blossoms. As I surveyed the progress daily, my mind often drifted to the thought of eating summer peaches right off the tree. I could almost taste the sweet juice dripping down my chin.

But just after the peaches set, a tornado came through and it was much too close for comfort. It didn't do any structural damage, but it blew all but one peach off our tree.

The peach looks lonesome hanging there. Jilda and I are trying to figure out who gets the peach. I could probably arm wrestle her for it, but with all the yoga she does, she's curiously strong now and I'm not sure if I can take her. Maybe she will consider sharing it with me.

We planted cabbage this year, but we were about a month late. The plants seemed to do fairly well until, one day when I was inspecting them, I saw a few small holes that had appeared almost overnight. Upon a closer look, I saw a tiny worm munching happily away on our cabbage. I gently picked him off and thumped him into the compost pile.

We went out of town for a few days and when we returned, all the cabbages had more holes than a flour sifter. This time when I picked the worms off, I stomped them with my tennis shoes. But more worms came back and soon our sad little cabbages whistled when the wind blew.

I pulled them all up by the roots and threw them in the compost bin to put them out of their misery.

We've had even worse luck with our chickens. A month ago we had a yard full of chickens. We'd awake each morning to the sound of Henry the Rooster telling us the news. I'm guessing our late-sleeping neighbors called him something else, but we loved old Henry.

Then, one morning Henry disappeared. There were a few feathers near the fence, but other than that not a trace of our rooster.

We had a mama hen with a brood of chicks that were still in the nest. The next morning, we found that our hen had been mauled and all the chicks but one were gone.

The next two days, the varmint ate all our chickens but one.
I did some research and narrowed the predator down to a couple of suspects. I was certain it was either a possum or a raccoon.

I bought a humane trap and the next night the puzzle was solved. I caught a raccoon that was as big as a Ford Focus.

That critter had a cute face, but when I picked up the cage, it lunged for my hand from inside the cage. It sounded like a Bengal tiger. I promptly dropped the cage and went to the shed to fetch my leather gloves.

I relocated the chicken slayer to Cullman County near the Mulberry River.

I felt so good about my conquest that I went to Jasper Seed and Feed and bought six more baby chicks.

The next morning when I went down to check the crib, all six chicks were gone. Apparently my striped friend had other family members who had heard about the Watson Chick-Fil-A.

I bought sardines, and cat food for critter bait. The next morning I had Rocky Raccoon Number 2.

Jilda asked, "Is that the same raccoon?" I wasn't sure if he'd found his way home or not, so to be sure, I took a can of spray paint and painted some nifty blue racing stripes on his butt.

I'm not buying any more chickens until I'm sure I have relocated the entire family somewhere far away.

Even with all my missteps, I'm still living a dream. Last night as we sat down to our first meal of fried green tomatoes, squash, and new potatoes with fresh peppers, a gentle rain began to fall. By the time dessert was on the table, a "gully-washer" had swept away a row of purple hull peas.

The Oak Ridge Boys summed it up well, I think, when they sang "If you're ever gonna see a rainbow, you got to stand a little rain."

S·E·V·N·T·E·E·N

Father's Day

My dad loved the water. He didn't care if he caught
a lot of fish, because to him it wasn't about the fish, but the
fishing. It was about being outside, far from the industrial fans
and the flying ash of his welding rod.

He wasn't a welder because he loved his work. He was
a welder because he needed to feed his family. He left his tools
at work because he wanted to keep that separate from his home
life.

The river was an escape from the mind-numbing
tedium of his job, and he spent a lot of time on the Warrior.
He loved it so much that he saved his money and eventually
bought a small lot by the water down in Rocky Hollow.

We then started scrounging around for building
supplies, and cobbled together a two-room cabin that by today's
standards would be considered a shack. But to us, it was like a
palace.

Later on, he saved up and bought a 14 foot V-bottom
aluminum boat with a ten-horse Wizard motor which was built
by Mercury, as I recall. It didn't have gears, so you had to be

mindful when you cranked that baby up or you'd find yourself in the river. It was a very small motor, but it made our boat scoot.

One sunny July day in 1964, dad and I went fishing and he let me drive the boat. It didn't have a steering wheel, so you had to sit at the back of the boat and steer by holding onto a throttle handle. If you wanted to go right, you had to pull the handle to the left and if you wanted to turn left, you pushed to the right.

That took some getting used to, but I quickly mastered it and from that day forward my dad rarely steered if I was in the boat. Dad was a patient and understanding man, which was fortunate for me. On my maiden voyage as a captain, I headed down the river at full speed. Dad sat in the front and pointed out logs floating just beneath the surface. I got good at dodging.

I was doing great when, all of a sudden, he stood up. He saw something in the water that I had missed. He shouted back over the noise of the screaming outboard motor "TURN AROUND". "WHAT?" I shouted back. "THERE'S A BIG SNAKE BACK THERE, TURN AROUND."

Daddy had seen a cottonmouth as big as a gator and he wanted to shoot it with his pistol. An experienced captain would have cut back on the throttle prior to the turning maneuver, but that's not what I did.

At top speed I shoved the steering handle hard to the right, which made the small boat veer to the left and tilt precariously to one side.

I fought to stabilize the boat and managed to keep it from capsizing. But unfortunately my dad was no longer standing in the bow of the boat. In fact, he wasn't in the boat at all, but in the river with a big ol' snake.

Fortunately, gravity kept the tackle box and most of the other gear in the boat so all I had to do was turn off the motor and paddle back to pick up my dad before he was eaten alive.

As I headed back for Dad, I kept a watchful eye out for the snake. Apparently, the splash (when Dad hit the water) had spooked the snake because it swam quickly toward the bank.

Once I realized that dad was not hurt, I fretted a little. I thought he'd be angry or, worse, that he would never let me drive the boat again.

When I reached down to help him back in the boat, he was smiling. He anchored his foot on the side of the boat and snatched me into the water head first. Then he laughed as hard as I've ever heard him laugh before. "If you don't like the water,' he said, "you have no business owning a boat."

Even today, whenever I go near the water, I think of my dad and that always makes me smile. Happy Father's Day.

E·I·G·H·T·E·E·N

Learning to Fish

My friend Dan Starnes invited me and another friend, Keith McCoy, to go fishing in Helen, Georgia last weekend. He'd rented a cottage and since he was taking his girlfriend, he asked if Jilda would like to come too.

I know for a fact that Jilda would rather have a root canal with a dull drill-bit than to fish, but I asked if she'd like to go and have some rest and relaxation at the cottage while the guys fished. She agreed, so the deal was done. She had second thoughts when she learned we'd have to leave after she got off work on Thursday evening – and we'd have to drive for five hours.

As it turns out, Dan's girlfriend is not that crazy about fishing either. So the girls toured north Georgia, ate, and shopped while we fished. I'm betting the lights dimmed in the American Express data center trying to process all the transactions they generated. But since we were having a large time, it was only fair that they have fun too. As is often said, "Fun ain't cheap."

We arrived at the Blackhawk Fly Fishing Camp before sunrise on Friday and were welcomed by the aroma of coffee wafting through the screen door of the hundred-year-old cabin. Off in the distance you could hear the Soque River rushing southward toward Helen, Georgia.

We drank coffee, chatted with our female guide, Deb Bowen, and got a game plan together. A few minutes later we suited up in our fly-fishing gear and waded out into the stream which was 41 degrees. My feet were soon like giant Popsicles but I was so excited to be on the water that it didn't bother me.

Both Dan and Keith are more accomplished fishermen than me, so they didn't spend much time listening to the guide telling them how to fish. With my first two casts, I caught the stump behind me and a rhododendron bush on the other bank. I figured out fairly quick that if I wanted to catch something besides vegetation, I'd better ask for help.

Deb was great – I didn't see her snicker once as she evaluated my technique. She made a few simple suggestions and after a little practice, I started putting the fly in the water -- which made it at least theoretically possible for me to catch a fish.

Deb is a retired IBM computer guru, who is now one of only a handful of certified fishing guides in the state of Georgia. She showed me how to read a stream, and how to put a fly in the best spot to catch a fish. She showed me the life cycle of the bugs on which the trout feed.

At the end of the day I'd learned a great deal, but I hadn't netted the first fish. This was unfortunate for the Rickster, because both Dan and Keith caught fish. I was the target of some fish barbs (pun intended).

On Saturday, I felt much more confident. I skillfully placed my flies in the right spot, and I hung a few fish within the first half hour, but I still wasn't landing them. Deb saw that I wasn't keeping enough tension on the line and with a few simple adjustments in my technique, I landed a rainbow trout about 13 inches long.

It wasn't a monster, but I was very encouraged. A few minutes later, I hung into a trout as big as a Honda Civic. It got away so I didn't really count it, but Deb and Keith saw it.

The fly-fishing rod and reel I use belonged to my dad. With it, he fished for bream and crappie down on the Warrior. To my knowledge, he never got a chance to go to a fancy cottage and spend the weekend fishing for rainbow trout. On Saturday, when the sun got high and cotton clouds drifted slowly across the sky, my thoughts turned to my dad.

I know he would have been proud that I got a chance to spend a beautiful weekend on the water and made good use of his old fishing rig – and happy that I caught a few rainbows.

N·I·N·E·T·E·E·N

Blackie and the Watermelon

The thermometer will be in the upper nineties this Fourth of July and Jilda is not happy. She keeps whining – why don't we summer in Telluride.

We fell in love with that place when we visited last year during the week of the Fourth. At noon, the temperature was in the low seventies with sunshine, and by nightfall, we had to wear light jackets to watch the fireworks.

The place was delightful. The weather, the people, the scenery, and the food was incredible. When our vacation was over, it was hard to board the plane to head back to the furnace we call home.

Did I mention that Jilda does NOT like hot weather? To her, the best thing about summer is watermelons and she hasn't had the best luck with them this year either.

We bought one this past week that weighed more than a Toyota. I almost "busted a gut" wagging that beast inside. I put it on the table near the air conditioning duct so that it would get good and cold.

Her thinking was that she'd get a big one, and share with her brother who lives next door. His family loves watermelon too, and sharing made sense because Jilda and I rarely eat 50 pounds of watermelon in one sitting.

I went fishing that morning, and since we were having company that evening, she wanted to change the table cloth. No problem because she's become curiously strong teaching all those yoga classes.

She moved the melon to the kitchen counter to put a new table cloth, and a bouquet fresh flowers on the table. She was arranging the flowers in the vase, and humming along with the stereo when all of a sudden she heard a loud SPLAT!!!

When she turned around, she saw the kitchen had a new avant-garde paint job. Watermelon was everywhere, including our dog Blackie, who unfortunately was in the kitchen eating. When she ran into the kitchen he was covered in red watermelon meat and seeds.

She said he just lay in the floor for a while licking the juice from his face. Finally he stood up and shook as if he'd just had a bath. This threw bits of melon to places that were originally untouched by the fruit calamity.

By the time I got home most of the mess in the house had been cleaned off the walls, the fridge, dishwasher, and cabinets, but the floor still felt a little tacky as I walked through.

I looked out the window into the back yard. She had Blackie in a #3 washtub spraying him off with a garden hose.

Blackie is about 12 years old, weighs about 100 pounds, and his fur is as thick as a mink coat, so he's not fond of summer either.

He seemed to be enjoying his bath, though it didn't appear to be as much fun for Jilda. Before it was over, she was soaked from head to toe. I didn't tease her because it was getting close to supper, and unless I wanted to eat sardines with saltines, I knew I'd better keep my mouth shut.

I also didn't mention the sticky kitchen floor. I did head back down to Jolly Chollie's produce stand to buy another watermelon that we could enjoy on the Fourth of July.

But then, I might wake up on the fourth with a note pinned to my pillow saying – "Blackie and I have gone to Telluride. We'll see you in September."

Happy Fourth of July.

T·W·E·N·T·Y

Home Depot

I've spent a lot of time in school during the course of my lifetime. You'd think with all that education, I'd be smart enough to resist even the most sophisticated marketing strategy. But when I go into a store like Lowes or The Home Depot, I REALLY get stupid.

The way these companies lay out the aisles is so clever. Every time I go to one of these super stores it's all I can do to keep from waving my arm expansively and saying to the sales person, "Yes, I'll take one of each of everything in this area here."

I drive a small truck, which helps my resistance because it can't hold that much stuff. But it seems the stores anticipated that little logistical issue by offering home delivery. I can hear them saying, "No problem sir, we'll use the BIG truck to deliver your stuff."

I spend hours looking at lighting, flooring, paint, fixtures, and the garden shop. The tools are another issue altogether. My wife has a "thang" for shoes, but my addiction may even be worse because I can never have too many tools.

Most men are helpless when it comes to managing tool ownership. I think it's in our DNA.

Whenever I'm doing a home project, I get a rush when I need a specific tool and realize that I have it hanging on a hook in my little shed. As I approach the tool section of Home Depot, I often find myself drooling.

It would be embarrassing, but whenever I go to one of these stores and look around, I'm never alone. Normally there are several other men looking lustfully at battery-operated saws, drills, nail guns, and air compressors.

You can hear the wheels turning in their minds: "I wonder if I could hide this from my wife? Sometimes she just scans the credit card statements. I might be able to slip by a $400 chipper/shredder," one might imagine them pondering.

It's comforting to know that I'm not the only one afflicted by this condition.

I was talking to a friend at work this past week. He was saying that he went into the local mega-hardware store to buy a roll of duct tape and came out $1,800 later with a new weed trimmer, drill set, a table saw, spray paint equipment, portable car battery booster, a new ceiling fan and a barbecue grill. Everything except duct tape.

His wife confiscated his Visa card and now forbids him to drive within a mile of a Lowes or The Home Depot. His family did an intervention and they are encouraging him to attend TA (Tool-a-holics Anonymous).

I shook my head solemnly in agreement, as I thought to myself, "Yes, I've shopped on that aisle before."

I know that for most men, there is an underlying reason for this infatuation with mega-hardware stores. We believe, deep down, that we are saving money by fixing things ourselves.

But hopefully, one day all men will come to understand this infatuation with mega-stores is a trap because each time we start a small home project, we inevitably need a roll of duct tape.

It's a vicious cycle.

T·W·E·N·T·Y~O·N·E

No Place Like Home

When I was younger, the last place I wanted to be was home. Back then I had this feeling in my gut that something was happening "out there" and I wanted to be part of it. I longed to feel a connection to something bigger; something exciting; something important!

I used to wish I lived in Atlanta, Nashville, New York, Chicago, or Los Angeles because in my mind, those places were closer to "the action".

I wanted to be some place where I could feel the pulse of the nation pounding through my chest like a rock drummer drinking espresso and popping diet pills. But instead, I was stuck at home.

One of my friends in the Army went to Woodstock. Many say Woodstock was the greatest music festival of all time. In August of 1969, my friend walked to the highway near his home, stuck out his thumb, and hitch-hiked to upstate New York.

He spent several days wandering around Max Yasgur's

600-acre farm in a drug stupor, trying to get his bearing. He said he kept asking people, "Where's the music?" They would point toward the setting sun and say "It's over there, and it's so beautiful!" He never found the stage, but years later when he told me the story, it still brought a smile to his face.

For someone who wanted to be close to the action, Woodstock sounded like the place to be in that particular moment in history.

I envied my wandering friend – well, not the drug-induced-stupor part, but the part about being somewhere exciting.

Something happens when you get older. Time and experience begin to shape your notion of what's important.

That's not to say that you shouldn't view life through the eyes of a child at every opportunity, because in order to stay young at heart, you have to keep an open mind and be amazed by simple things.

But if you're lucky, when you get older, you find your pace. You begin to understand that if you can't find happiness at home, you're probably not going to find it anywhere else either.

Last weekend, Jilda and I went to our great nephew Stone's birthday party in Adamsville, which is about 20 miles away. He was seven on Halloween and he had a crew of kids at his party.

Jordan is another great nephew who lives next door and spends every Tuesday and Thursday with Jilda and me. He went to the party too, but he felt out of place.

When he saw me, he ran over and reached up for me to pick him up. The night was chilly and he snuggled up close to me to get warm. When I asked if he was OK, he whispered, "I don't know anybody. I want to go home." I held him for a long while.

Later, when we got ready to leave, Jordan fell in step with me. It was his intention to head home. He had come with his Nanna, but if we'd had a car seat, he would have left with us.

Even at the tender age of two, he understood something that took me years to grasp: there is no place like home.

T·W·E·N·T·Y~T·W·O

Honor

Last Saturday was an interesting day in more ways than one. Weather-wise, you know you're in Alabama when you hear the weatherman say that the chances of large hail, dangerous lightning, flash floods, and catastrophic tornadoes is 100% today, 80% tonight, and 60% each day for the rest of your life.

They've downgraded the chances for plague, locusts, and pestilence from 50% this evening to 40% overnight. The earthquake and tsunami warnings have been lifted for now but it would be a good idea to sleep in your bike helmet and lifejacket. UFOs are expected in most trailer parks across central Alabama.

Like many of you, Jilda and I stayed close to home for most of the day and watched James Spann on TV. James, in my opinion, is the best weatherman on the planet.

When he looks at the map during these weather events, he not only gives you the path of the storm but he identifies landmarks and communities that aren't even on the map. I wouldn't be surprised to hear him say, "Hazel Jones, this storm is headed for Doliska, so you and Harold need to get your cat

Tiger and get down to the storm pit right now!"

Anyhow, on Saturday night, it was hard to tell if the weather was going to be bad for us here in Walker County. We had planned to go to the Dora High School all class reunion down at Bevill State, but I was leaning towards staying home.

I should have known that something was up when I asked Jilda if she wanted to go to the reunion. She's a weather watcher from way back and she normally errs on the side of caution when there's a chance of being blown to Atlanta in a funnel cloud, but Saturday night she said, yes, let's go.

We headed out, and when we arrived the parking lot was full. Apparently, there was a bunch of other people who thought the weather would be OK.

We had a great time visiting with all our old friends. Jilda's maiden name is Phillips, which makes her kin to most of the folks in Walker County, so these high school gatherings are almost like family reunions. The officers recognized each class. Bob Ellis, who graduated in the Forties, was the oldest classmate who attended.

Then Martha Burroughs began reading the intro for the Alumnus of the Year. I got my camera ready to snap the photograph, but as she read, something didn't sound right. It sounded almost like she was introducing me!

When the realization set in that she WAS talking about me, the blood began throbbing in my ears. I was shocked, to say the least. The reasons they cited for selecting me had to do with my work with the *Daily Mountain Eagle*, the book *Remembering Big*, my success with Jilda as singer/songwriters, the fact that Jilda and I do an annual scholarship for a deserving student, and my work on the Dora High School alumni website.

But it almost felt like cheating because I love the work I do. I started DoraHighSchool.com back in 2001. It was the first website I'd ever done and I had no idea whether anyone would visit the site or not. I soon discovered that they did visit, and word spread like wildfire.

The early success with that site, and the encouragement I received for my work, gave me courage to approach the *Eagle* about writing a weekly column and the book flowed from that.

On Saturday evening, I vaguely remember going to the podium to receive the award. I spoke for about five minutes, though I don't remember what I said.

Here's what I hope I said: I am flattered and humbled by this honor. I love my old school and I consider my time there a gift. My hope is that I can continue to do things that reflect well on my alma mater and my community.

T•W•E•N•T•Y~T•H•R•E•E

Our House Becomes a Jungle

Our house is a jungle! It happens every year when Jack Frost comes a-nipping outside. We have a yard full of tropical and semi-tropical plants that summer just beyond our living room windows. But in the fall at the mention of cold weather, we haul them inside.

When you walk into our house, you'll see lemon, orange, grapefruit, avocado, and mango trees as well as a ton of other plants that I challenge you to name.

Mammie, Jilda's grandma on her father's side of the family, had a modified storm pit that her grandpa built for storing plants in the winter. It was below ground, which kept the temperature stable. It had windows on the roof and in the door that allowed enough light in for the plants to survive until spring.

We don't have a room like that, so all our plants must come into our living room – which makes life interesting for several days after the move.

Cohabiting with our green friends is not easy.

Each winter when we bring them in, we have to rearrange our living space to make room for them. It takes weeks for me to stop kicking pots and getting poked in the eye by low-hanging limbs.

It's not uncommon, when we move the plants inside, to bring in "guests" who've made their summer homes in our greenery. Tree frogs, chameleons, spiders, and all kinds of bugs have, at one time or the other, come in with our plants.

Once a burrowing chipmunk, hidden among the roots of our giant philodendron, found himself trapped inside.

I worked with MaBell at the time and I got a frantic call from Jilda who was standing on the kitchen table with our niece Samantha who was five at that time.

Apparently the tiny striped squirrel had come out to forage for food in the den, and had an unfortunate encounter with the girls. The two were held hostage by a menacing quadruped that was not much bigger than a well-fed mouse.

I listened helplessly on the phone line as Jilda tried to shoo the little bugger out. He mounted an unexpected counter-offensive, and it was not going well for the home team.

They left the front door open, and the tiny beast finally scurried out screeching and chattering. Jilda and Samantha were both convinced that the chipmunk had said unkind things about their lineage as he darted by them.

But these close encounters with the natural world are a small price to pay for an indoor greenroom.

Plants kind of grow on you (pun intended). We've had some of ours for many years. I have a fichus plant that my friends at work sent when my father passed away in 1986.

Jilda has a plant that belonged to her grandmother, that was full grown when Granny gave it to Ruby (Jilda's mom) in 1964 when Lyndon Johnson was president. The citrus trees were all planted from seed by Ruby.

I really need to build a plant room suitable for our plants to thrive and survive when the mercury plunges. I'll put that on my ever-expanding to-do list. But tonight, we're in the living room listening for jungle sounds and on the lookout for "guests".

T·W·E·N·T·Y~F·O·U·R

Observations on Child Rearing

I've spent a lot of time in shopping malls, promoting and signing books. In between customers, I like to people-watch. As Yogi Berra once said, "You can observe a lot, just by watching."

One day I saw a kid misbehaving in a major way, and I thought how different his life would be, had he grown up around my mother.

This boy was about five years old, and two feet tall, but he made up for it in loudness. He apparently wanted something from the toy store, and he was letting everyone in the mall know it.

Both the parents were in a tizzy. "I can't do a thing with you!" the mother whined. I wondered to myself, if she can't do anything with him now, what is she going to do when he's a teenager, and still behaving badly?

I'm a problem-solver by nature, and I considered whether one of those shock collars used to train misbehaving bird-dogs might be an option.

My mother always has helpful suggestions on child discipline too. This much is for sure -- "I don't know what to do with him!" is not a phrase that she ever used.

When one of us kids misbehaved in public, she took a two-phased approach. The first was her Vulcan mind-meld stare. When she locked eyes with you, she had the uncanny ability to bypass your ears and speak directly into your soul: "Just wait till I get you home!"

At that point, you knew beyond a shadow of doubt that no good things would happen when you reached home. Phase two discipline--for more serious infractions--was immediate, and involved the nearest tree, shrub, or leather object.

We had a distant cousin from up north who came to visit one summer. He was a naturally rowdy kid who had run wild for most of his life. One warm summer day we were riding bikes in the backyard. Mother had just washed a fresh load of white sheets, and they hung on the line blowing like flags in the warm breeze.

She called to us through an open window in a normal tone of voice, "Boys, don't ride too near the clothesline, or you'll get up against the sheets." That was enough information for me. I pointed my bike toward the front yard. But Bobby (not his real name) made one last pass, and held out his dirty hand to touch the sheets as he rode by.

I heard our back screen door slap hard against the jamb, and fast-moving footsteps coming from the direction of the house. I never liked that sound one bit.

Mama snagged a keen hickory from a nearby peach tree and made a beeline for Bobby. He was a cocky boy, and I heard him say defiantly, "You ain't my mama!"

With a move as quick as a grizzly catching a salmon, she snatched him off the bicycle and gave him about five quick lashes across the legs with the hickory. She used her mind-meld technique, looked into his eyes, and said in a slow, measured voice, "When you're in MY yard, I'm your mama." Bobby, who was not accustomed to ill treatment, took it hard and headed home on his bike.

The unfortunate thing for Bobby was that his grandmother lived nearby and had seen what just went down. Not wanting to be outdone by my mother, she grabbed a limb off a hedge bush, snatched Bobby up by the collar and striped his legs some more.

Although it was a weekend, that day was a school day for Bobby. He learned his lesson well. From that day forward, he always said "please?" and "thank you" to my mama, whether he was in her yard or not.

So when I saw the five-year-old misbehaving at the

mall and heard the young mother say, "I can't do a thing with him," I had to restrain myself from suggesting she contact my mom. I'm sure her advice would have been very helpful.

T·W·E·N·T·Y~F·I·V·E
Some Lessons Come Hard

Anybody who thinks their education ends the day they walk out of high school might as well be smoking dope, because they couldn't be more clueless.

When you leave high school (or college), life's teachers take over and they can be harsh. In the school of life, you get the test BEFORE you get the lesson.

These lessons can be quite expensive, because if you don't learn the first time, you get to take the course again and again, until you learn it. Yes, I'm here to tell you, every day's a school day.

This week's lesson came when I tried to install a new dishwasher. Let me start at the beginning.

We've had our old dishwasher for years, and we've washed a train load of dirty dishes. But earlier this week, when I opened the door to take out the clean dishes, the bottom was full of nasty water that smelled like we'd washed a rat that had been dead for a week.

When I did the math, I realized the dishwasher was about 12 years old so it seemed reasonable to me that it needed replacing. The search for a new one began.

I priced a few units in Birmingham, and I found some in our range, but I prefer doing business closer to home, so I ran by the local appliance store, and I found the unit we wanted. With a swipe of a debit card and a handshake, we were on the way home.

My brother-in-law, who is a master plumber, offered to help. But he stays busy, and I hated to bother him. I decided to install the new dishwasher myself – STRIKE ONE.

I removed the screws that secured the old unit to the cabinet, and I began to slide it back and forth to get it out. All of a sudden, I heard something snap. I thought to myself, this can't be good. A moment later, a hidden copper pipe was gushing hot water like a fire hydrant.

I'd forgotten to turn off the water valve BEFORE I started the replacement. In an instant, I was sloshing around in ankle-deep water, and my mind felt as if I had a head full of cold molasses. I couldn't remember where our cutoff valve was. – STRIKE TWO.

When my brain finally decided to join me, I dashed to the shed, snatched up a crescent wrench, and ran toward the water cutoff valve down by the mailbox. It would have appeared, from a distance, that I'd stepped in a yellow-jacket nest.

When I got back inside, the water was almost deep enough to water ski . Jilda fetched all the towels in the closet and began drying the floors.

About that time, she phoned her brother, and asked him to come over to assist me. He walked in shaking his head knowingly. But in a matter of minutes he analyzed the situation, and we were in the truck heading to the plumbing-supply store to get parts.

The rest of the job went smoothly, and soon we were loading the new dishwasher for its maiden voyage. I listened intently to all the clicks and whirrs of the new unit, and I found myself smiling.

The smile quickly vanished when I opened up the new dishwasher to unload the clean dishes and found the bottom full of water, just like the old unit.

As it turns out, a $10 air valve in the sink, through which the dishwasher drains, had clogged and caused the problem – STRIKE THREE.

So, what did life teach the Rickster today? Well, I learned NOT to assume. I learned to take time for due diligence, and isolate problems BEFORE digging deep into my wallet to buy unneeded appliances. And, if a professional offers you help, take it.

T·W·E·N·T·Y~S·I·X

Time Moves On

When you're young you think you'll live forever and age is such a foreign and distant concept. I can remember when I was 20, trying to imagine myself at 60 and I simply could not conjure up an image.

Never would I have believed that my hair would have gone south, and to be frank, I'm still a little peeved about that. But all in all, life has been good to Jilda and me. We busied ourselves with our daily routines -- working, studying, writing songs, and playing music; time moved on.

Things weren't always easy, and money was often tight in the early years, but we managed. We both worked two jobs at times, and found a way to make ends meet.

Later we went to night school and got some degrees. Gradually our job situations began to improve. We built a new house and moved out of our cozy little mobile home....actually, snug might be a better way of describing the trailer.

We planted flowers and fruit trees, and turned the new house into a home; time moved on.

I think Jilda and I got along better than most. That's

not to say there weren't times she got so angry with me that she could have carved me up with a butcher knife and left me twitching in the laundry hamper with the wet towels and dirty socks.

There were times I fantasized about a similar fate for her, but those times were few. We learned to say "I'm sorry" and time moved on.

We were fortunate because my job with MaBell gave us an opportunity to travel all over the country on business. Jilda often traveled with me to San Francisco, Seattle, Boston, Atlanta, Miami, Mobile, New Orleans, and Arizona as well as other places.

We continued doing the things we loved. We made new friends, played music, and grew up together. I'm not sure we expressed enough gratitude, but time moved on.

Then a few weeks ago a doctor's visit fired a shot across our bow. Jilda was sick with all kinds of bugs and infections for most of 2011. She'd gone in for yet another lung infection, and the pulmonary doctor found something abnormal in her blood work that hadn't shown up before.

He was a little vague about what it meant, instead he referred her to another doctor. When we looked up the new doc, it turns out she is an oncologist/hematology specialist.

WHAT?

You would not believe the kinds of things your mind can conjure up when it's not sure what you're up against. It took a few long days to get an appointment.

I went in for the visit too, and as we sat in the examining room there were those medical posters hanging around that explained about lung cancer and its implications.

When the doctor came in and began talking about her findings, I blurted out – does she have cancer? I breathed a sigh of relief when she said no. There is still a problem with Jilda's immune system they have yet to pinpoint, but it sounds like it's treatable. We'll know more in the coming week after more tests.

The lesson that we've both learned is that it's too easy to let days, weeks, months and years slip by unnoticed – uncelebrated. Time moves like a leaf on a slow-moving river and it's our intention to never forget this fact.

T•W•E•N•T•Y~S•E•V•E•N

Littering

One new chore I've assigned myself these days is litter patrol in my neighborhood. Thanks to some of our neighbors and their guests, we always have an abundance of litter casually tossed from passing cars.

It's not a problem confined to my area, because I see litter and garbage by the roadside almost everywhere I go in Alabama.

I've been behind people at red lights that actually put their cars in park, open their doors, and dump an ashtray full of cigarette butts right there in the street.

I wonder what gave them the idea that this is acceptable behavior? I guess they think that cigarette butts are not really litter, "since they are biodegradable." I actually believe that plutonium would break down and become safe for the environment quicker than a cigarette filter. Those butts will still be in the gutter when the sun runs out of gas and the moon turns into Swiss cheese.

I, for one, think it's OK for policemen to taser anyone they catch doing the dump-and-run routine. I'm not talking about doing any serious damage, but hit them with enough voltage to make them wet their britches and cause a permanent condition that makes them twitch involuntarily whenever they hear the word litter.

I think the fine in Walker County is $25 and has the same priority as prosecuting those who tear the labels off mattresses.

I really think the penalty for littering should not be money, but sixteen hours of supervised community service, where the violators must pick up roadside litter for a weekend. It would be best if they had to perform the community service in their own communities to maximize the embarrassment when friends and neighbors see them on garbage patrol.

As bad as littering is, there are much worse offenders. It's those degenerates who dump dead animals by the side of the road that galls me most.

There is a wide place in the road on the way to our house and we find a variety of dead creatures dumped there constantly. It's common to see dogs, cats, and other critters tossed out. Have these folks never heard of a shovel?

During hunting season this past year, someone had cut the heads off two deer and dumped the carcasses there for our community to enjoy. I'm telling you, these folks must have crawled from the shallow end of the gene pool.

All the hunters I know find this as disturbing as I do, and would readily endorse the taser treatment I mentioned above for the offenders.

I can write until my fingers are blue, and this problem will not go away. In reality, I don't think fines are the answer. It takes a dummy to litter, but most of them are smart enough to wait until the patrol car behind them turns off before they toss an empty bottle out the window.

I think the answer to this problem is early education, and teaching kids to have a sense of pride in one's community and state. Then, perhaps they'd take better care of the planet than their parents.

I know you may say with all the problems we face in this country today, why are you wasting energy on the problem of litter?

Well, the thing is, you can't fix all the problems at once, but you have to start somewhere. Why not start here at home?

T·W·E·N·T·Y~E·I·G·H·T

Looking Without Seeing

Have you ever listened to a radio when the knob was a little off the station? The music gets lost in the noise and you don't even realize that you're hearing without listening.

These days it seems my life is filled with static and it affects all my senses.

I read an interview with Michael Gelb, the author who wrote, How to Think like Leonardo Da Vinci. The great artist once said, "People look without seeing, hear without listening, eat without awareness of taste, touch without feeling, and talk without thinking." It's almost 600 years later and this quote seems even more true today.

I think, to some extent, we are casualties of the modern world and the velocity of information. Einstein's theory should say, the only thing that travels faster than the speed of light is life in the 21st century.

It seems the faster you run, the farther you fall behind. Most of us try to jam 25 hours into each 24-hour day. At this pace, life can be a blur. But it doesn't have to be this way.

Life is remarkable in unexpected ways. One of my newsletters talked about life around us. "Even cities are teeming with life: birds, bees, chipmunks and squirrels are all around, but are seldom seen."

This past week I woke up before daybreak feeling anxious from all the things on my to-do list. I put on a pot of coffee and stepped out on the back deck to get the "local forecast". A gentle breeze out of the southwest stirred the wind chimes, and I took a moment to contemplate my life and whatnot.

When I realized how nice it felt, I stepped inside to get a couch pillow and a blanket, before settling in on the antique glider. My knees squeaked as I folded them into a seated yoga position, but the pain subsided after a few moments and I began to focus on my breathing.

Off in the distance I heard a rooster crowing, which came to the attention of our roosters, and soon there was a crowing contest. The sound of a commercial jet five miles overhead swept through my aural landscape and it was like listening to the lead part in the song, "All Along the Watchtower" by Jimi Hendrix.

It was a cool effect that I had not noticed in years. I thank the stillness for this gift.

I think it's moments like those that help me to stop being a spectator in life and become a participant.

The next time you get a chance to go for a walk, try walking outside instead of inside on a treadmill. If you have a small camera, take it with you. As you walk, be mindful of the sights and sounds around you. Try to "see" the seasonal slide show brought to you by Mother Nature.

Find something to photograph. Forget about work, forget about the bills, forget about the chores, and just "be there" in the moment. Try to use every one of your senses.

If you're like me, you'll begin to "see" life in new and interesting ways.

T·W·E·N·T·Y~N·I·N·E

Midnight Snacker

I woke up after midnight last week and I couldn't go back to sleep. I'd been in the middle of a good dream, but once my eyes opened, it vanished like a wisp of breath on a cold morning.

I tossed and turned for a while, but my mind kept searching for the dream. I finally got up and headed for the kitchen. Jilda had cooked black-eyed peas, corn on the cob, and cornbread for dinner that evening.

I reached for one of our vintage drinking glasses from the cupboard. It's one that Jilda inherited from her mother, and it's heavy enough to use as a weapon. In fact, her mother told her that if I ever got out of line, she could clobber me with one of those glasses, and I'd be drinking through a straw for months. That thought still lingers in the back of my mind.

Anyhow, I crumbled up a wedge of cornbread into the glass, and finished filling it with cold buttermilk. I stood there in my PJs and ate my midnight snack by refrigerator light.

I know with the cost of energy, I should be more mindful about wasting cold air, but it's a habit I picked up from my dad.

He was a "midnight snacker" too. As I've mentioned before, my mama cooked beans for supper every night. Most of the time they were butterbeans, but she did cook pintos, and navy beans too.

Dad's favorite midnight snack was cold butterbeans with a thick slice of onion, on two slices of light bread. He'd chase it with buttermilk. He too would snack by the light of the old Frigidaire.

As I ate, I tried to think of the earliest memory of my dad. The one that came to mind was when we lived in the old house in Sloss.

That must have been before underpinning, because the front porch of that old house was about four feet off the ground, but at the back it sat so low that only dogs and small kids could get under there.

This particular day, Dad was looking for the rubber pull-handle that attached to the end of the crank cord on his old Wizard outboard motor. It was springtime and he was getting his boat ready for fishing. The crank cord had broken back in the winter and he'd decided to wait until spring to fix it.

He looked high and low for the handle but it had vanished. I was about four years old at the time. I was shoeless, shirtless, and skinny as a kid from a third-world country. When Dad described what he was looking for, I knew immediately where it was.

I scooted underneath the low part of the house like a chipmunk with an acorn. About midway under the house, the pull handle was lying right next to the clothespin Army men, and the brick road scraper. Apparently one of our hounds had snatched the handle and used it for a chew toy.

When I scurried out from under the house with the pull-handle, my dad smiled broadly at me. He reached down, picked me up, and tossed me into the air. I squealed with delight. He patted me on the head and told my Uncle Elmer, "That's my buddy." I don't know that I've ever felt more proud.

I smiled at the memory. Then I rinsed my glass out in the sink, closed the fridge, and went back to bed.

I think I was asleep before my head hit the pillow. Sometimes a memory is better than a good dream. Happy Father's Day.

T·H·I·R·T·Y

Miracle in Sloss Hollow

Each year, beginning the first week of December, Jilda and I take time to watch our collection of Christmas movies. We absolutely love "The Bishop's Wife", "It's a Wonderful Life", and "Miracle on 34th Street."

Last night we watched "Christmas Vacation," which is a scream. One poignant scene in the movie is when the Chevy Chase character, Clarke Griswold, is watching old 8mm films of past family Christmases.

We have those old films and videos too. I've watched them many times and, like Clarke, they put a smile on my face, and at times, they moved me to tears.

It's interesting what people remember about Christmas at my mom and dad's house. To folks driving through our old neighborhood it would probably be the yard-full of decorations that went up the Friday after Thanksgiving.

The whole neighborhood got into an "exterior illumination" contest and it was not uncommon during the weeks before Christmas to need a policeman to direct traffic in the neighborhood because of all the people driving through to see the lights.

To the younger kids, grandkids, nieces, nephews, and other members of our extended family, the memory would probably be the mountains of gifts under my mama's Christmas tree.

But for me, it's that old movie in my mind of my mama in her kitchen during the weeks before Christmas.

When she was home, she spent the month of December making divinity candy, fudge, pecan pies, banana nut bread, and German chocolate cakes. She made chocolate marshmallow treats, peanut butter candy, and sweet-potato pies. When I close my eyes, I can almost taste the Christmas punch she made.

She had wire-bound notebooks full of handwritten recipes for confections and baked goods that would be worth a fortune to most candy companies.

When we'd visit mama's kitchen, Jilda had to be restrained to keep her from diving head first onto the table and eating her way through.

Mama made more sweet stuff than her friends and family could eat. Those rewarded with sweets included kids, grandkids, nieces, nephews, cousins, neighbors, and people whose last names started with W.

If you didn't leave her house at Christmastime with a sugar buzz, it was probably because you were unconscious when you arrived.

That was my mama in her element. It was something that gave her joy. Her work in her kitchen was more like play.

Some years back my mom started having issues with her health, which forced her to abandon an independent lifestyle and move in with my older sister. I consider my older sister an angel. I know her life changed dramatically when my mom went to live with her. But she welcomed my mom into her home, and has provided care that no amount of money can buy.

Through the years, I think my mom harbored hopes that someday she would get to go back home and spend Christmas in her kitchen baking cakes and goodies for all the people she loved. I wish she could do that too.

With all the talk about magic at Christmas, here's some magic I'd love to see. I'd love to have all my family and friends together in the old house at Christmas with my mama moving about the kitchen like a dancer, frosting cakes and cutting chunks of fudge as big as bricks.

The movie could be called "Miracle in Sloss Hollow." Merry Christmas.

T·H·I·R·T·Y~O·N·E

I Miss My Brothers

February for me is always a little sad. My baby brother, who died in 2000, was born on February 15, and my older brother Neil died February 13, 1994. Both were way too young to lose and I've never really gotten over the loss.

My baby brother Darrin was 14 years younger than me, and I left home a few years after he was born. So due to the age difference, we didn't have as much history as I had with my older brother Neil. He was about seven years older than me, which was just the right age to keep me in line.

He was a good kid, but he had a mean streak that came out now and then. My parents bought him a Benjamin Franklin pellet gun when he was about 16 and he immediately proclaimed himself god over the other kids in the neighborhood. Not THE God, but in those days he was the god of firepower, and anyone who didn't like it could talk to Mr. Franklin.

If he pumped that thing up five or six times, he probably could have brought down an elk, but when you pumped it once or twice, it would only leave a nasty whelp if he popped you on the rear end. He used this mode for behavior management.

One spring day after he got Ol' Ben, I was being a total pain and Neil decided it was time for a little attitude adjustment. He pumped a little air in the chamber and popped me on my left thigh with Ol' Ben. It felt like I had gotten stun by a hornet. I headed straight for the house to rat him out to mother.

She was judge and jury in such matters and while she often fought back the urge to choke me herself, she took a dim view of his approach to behavior modification. I knew in fact that she would make him pay dearly.

Neil headed me off at the pass and tried to derail my mission. "Come on, you little baby! That didn't hurt!" he sneered. I could often be swayed when my maturity was questioned, but I was undeterred. My mom was on the back porch feeding blue jeans through the wringer of the old Maytag washer. Washing clothes always made her irritable for some reason.

I knew when I delivered the news about the shooting, she would serve up a fresh helping of hickory tea for Neil.

"If you tell mama, she'll hit the roof," he said with a little desperation in his voice. "You got that right, bubba," I agreed, knowing that justice was about to be served.

He changed tactics and said with a hint of malice, "If I get a whuppin, I'll catch you sleeping one night and put a grub worm in your ear. It will eat out your brains and all your wiring and you'll spend the rest of your life walking around like a zombie."

Now, I had seen my share of Saturday morning zombies on the old Motorola and I felt an involuntary shiver race up my spine when I thought about that grub worm munching on my medulla. I was pretty sure he was bluffing, but that threat put a nasty picture in my head. I actually had bad dreams for a month afterward. I decided to give him another chance.

This evening I felt a little melancholy when I sat down to write, but remembering this story brought a smile to my face. And even though it's been several years since they passed on, I still miss my brothers.

T•H•I•R•T•Y~T•W•O

Home

We got around early this morning and walked before the sun got up above the trees. Even without the sun, the morning was already hot and the humidity hung on our skin like a wet kiss from one of our big ol' goofy dogs.

When we got back in, we did a quick spruce-up in the house because we'd invited our friends over for dinner. Jilda stepped down to her flower garden and cut some daisies, black-eye Susans, some old maids, and a few gardenias for an arrangement on the table and in the guest bathroom.

That evening a thunder storm slammed its way down from the north and rattled the china in our cupboard. All the dogs tried to get in our laps. As I've mentioned before, we have some BIG dogs. Even though they are big, they are all big wusses when it comes to thunder – except for Taylor. She's the bulldog mix that weighs more than our Frigidaire, and she wouldn't be afraid of Satan on a mean drunk.

When the rain came, it was falling so hard it looked like a heavy fog out in the fields and I could barely see the apple tree. Thankfully, the deluge slacked enough for our company to run inside before it commenced again. After hours of sun as hot as a coal stove, the plants seemed to be dancing in the rain.

We visited with our friends for a while, and played some music on the old guitars before dinner.

Jilda had cooked baked chicken, broasted potatoes, and lima beans. For desert we had blackberry pie with homemade vanilla ice cream. For a long time all you could hear from the dining room was grunting. My spouse is one fine cook and she can silence even the rowdiest crowd with her cooking.

Four deer came up in the garden and put on a show while we ate. Two of the deer are young and they played a game of freeze tag. I love it when they do that.

The deer show does have a downside. This spring they ate our peas and beans faster than we could plant them, but I guess all good entertainment comes at a price.

After dinner we sat around and "talked until our tongues got tired" (as Dan Fogelberg once sang).

When our friends left, I helped Jilda clean up the kitchen and we sat out on the screen porch. The rain had moved off to the east, but you could still hear the ticking of rain drops falling off oak leaves onto our metal roof. It almost put me to sleep.

The sun had already dipped below the horizon, but there was enough lingering light to paint the sky a color of pink/purple that I can find no words to describe. I grabbed my camera and snapped a picture, but no camera can do justice to an evening sky.

There really is no place like home, especially on days like today. You could spend a fortune and travel halfway around the world and not have as good a time as I've had today, right here at home.

T·H·I·R·T·Y~T·H·R·E·E

Screened Porch

Last Sunday morning I woke up early and lay in bed silently going over my "grateful list." I could hear thunder off in the distance. The promise of rain was enough to persuade me to get up and check out the morning sky.

I put on a pot of coffee and stepped out to the screen porch to sit a while. The wind was out of the southwest making the chimes tinkle softly. Mourning Doves cooed in the pines, waiting for Jilda to toss out a few scoops of corn. I could smell the rain moving in and I made a mental note to add our screen porch to my list of things for which I am grateful.

Several years ago, we made the decision to do some home improvements. We built a small room for the washer and dryer and we made it large enough for a love seat and our TV. We realized that we were watching too much television and decided to make the activity less convenient.

The smartest thing we did during the construction phase was to build a screened porch. It quickly became one of our favorite parts of our home. It has a ceiling fan, Adirondack chairs, a small round tile-topped patio table, and a waist-high statue of Saint Francis who keeps an eye on the place from the corner.

We leave a string of white Christmas lights around the top of the porch year around, and at night, it looks like something from a fairy tale.

We have twelve sets of wind chimes hanging all around the porch and the song we hear depends upon the direction of the wind.

A few weeks ago, Jilda and I were having our morning coffee on the porch when we noticed a small sparrow inside the screen. It was a little Sunday morning gift. But then I realized our ceiling fan was spinning which could hurt the tiny creature if it got spooked. I jumped up and cut the fan off before we tried to figure out what to do with the bird.

When the fan stopped spinning I moved to open the screen door to allow the bird an escape path. But the tiny creature simply dropped down to the floor near the switch for our fountain, and scooted out a tiny tear in the screen. I thought to myself, she didn't just now figure that out.

I started looking around the porch. Nothing was out of the ordinary, until I looked up to the rack where I store my fly rods. I saw a small heart-shaped wicker basket that Jilda had hung on the rack.

A closer look revealed bits of straw hanging from the basket. I pulled a chair over to get a better look. When I leaned in close, I whistled a little tweeting sound and three tiny heads poked up towards the opening of the nest.

Jilda stood in the chair to have a look for herself and suddenly we heard mama sparrow fussing at us from the Rose-of-Sharon bush next to the porch. I'm sure if we had an aviary translator, we would have heard some unflattering thing about us and our ancestors.

When I was growing up, screened porches were really common. Neighbors often stopped by in the evening to catch up on the latest community news. Maybe it's nostalgia that makes our porch seem so special. It's hard to say for sure, but I know it's some of the best money I've ever spent.

T·H·I·R·T·Y~F·O·U·R

Power Outage

We camped this week without leaving the house. I knew we were in for an interesting time when I watched the local TV weatherman last Thursday. He was pointing excitedly to a big glob of red and yellow stuff on the radar map and jabbering like a spider monkey, about spring cold fronts and moisture coming in from the Gulf.

I normally pay attention, but predicting the weather accurately is like trying to pick next week's Powerball numbers.

As it turns out, he was right this time because a front moved in Friday night and promptly blew our lights to somewhere in South Carolina. We have huge trees in our yard and the wind made them sway like a barmaid listening to Elvis on the jukebox.

I have Alabama Power on speed dial, because the service out where we live can be spotty at times. I was on the phone to their computer before the shadows faded from the walls.

The repairmen arrived before the chickens got up and they had our lights on in time for our morning coffee.

We'd planned to plant our garden Saturday, but that darn weatherman was back on the tube saying we hadn't seen the last of the bad weather and it was going to get cold again. So we sharpened our garden tools and drooled while browsing through our seed catalogs.

Easter Sunday was a beautiful morning, and while we were reading our morning paper I glanced out the front windows and noticed a tiny squirrel scampering down the power line. Otherwise it was still as a painting outside. At that moment, the power went off again. Now, I'm not saying the squirrel caused the outage. But you have to admit it was an interesting accident.

A while later, a technician showed up and reset the fuse up the road. I wanted to offer up the dancing squirrel idea as the root cause of the outage, but feared he might take a dim view of my theory and leave my lights off until Christmas.

Fast forward to Sunday night/Monday morning: distant thunder woke us up. I listened as the sound of the wind got louder and louder. You could hear limbs cracking and debris rattling against the side of the house. Before the wind died down, our lights were out again for the third time in three days. I had a sinking feeling that the fix this time would take more than a few hours.

When I called in, you could tell their system was in overdrive. I got the definite impression that the computer which normally sounds friendly and cheerful, wanted to say "get in line, Bubba. You'll get juice when we get to you!"

I took off work on Monday and headed to the station to get gas for the generator. On the way out, I passed by downed power and cable TV lines.

I drove about ten miles to find a station that had electricity, and bought enough gas to feed the small generator for several days. The unit is only big enough to keep the fridge and freezer working.

Just before I left for work on Tuesday morning the phones, which depend on electricity to keep the batteries in the repeater boxes charged, died. So at that point, we had no power, no cable TV and no phones.

Later, I was eating lunch at my desk when Jilda called. She had headed out on errands and called to say, "I have some good news and some bad news."

"Alabama Power is working on the lines on our road," she said mirthfully. I waited for the other shoe to drop. "But apparently some of the work crews got off the edge of the road and broke the water main. Water is shooting up 30 feet into the air," she said, laughing hysterically. It struck me funny too and I spewed tea all over my desk and laughed until I had tears in my eyes.

So at that point, the situation was: we had no power, no cable, no phones or water. I told her to keep an eye out for locusts or other pestilence in the area.

It's funny now, but I know these "weather events" are no fun for all the utility people who work day and night to get our lives back to normal. I want to say thanks to them all for all their hard work. We now have water, phones, and lights. Our cable TV is still not on but we've decided to do what we do when we go camping, and read instead.

T·H·I·R·T·Y~F·I·V·E

RIP Flossy

I know that nobility, bravery, and sacrifice are not words you would normally associate with chickens. I've been around chickens all my life, and for the most part I've never given them much thought. But over the past couple of weeks I've come to see them in a different light.

Some time back, a neighbor who was renting a place across the road from us raised game chickens. A few of his chickens fled the captivity of his yard and into the sanctuary of our yard. Two hens began roosting in our huckleberry bush. When the sun struck their feathers, they turned amber like an expensive Persian rug.

The day the guy moved, he came over after dark for his chickens. As he approached the huckleberry bush, the hens bailed out and ran around the yard with this guy in hot pursuit. If I had filmed the episode, I could have won first place in America's Funniest Videos because it was a scream.

He was a smoker and after chasing the chickens for about 20 minutes, he could not take the exertion or the fact that we were laughing uncontrollably at his plight. He stomped out his cigarette and said "you can keep the dang chickens" (he used the bad word). So we did.

Some time later, we got a rooster to go with the hens and they've kept all the ants and bugs pecked up out of our yard.

A few weeks ago, Flossy had her first batch of chicks. One morning we saw six tiny peeps following her around our yard, scratching and pecking the ground.

Flossy was a warrior-mother at heart. She took guff from nothing or no one. She weighed about five pounds soaking wet, but she looked a lot bigger when she was mad.

A dog that lives down the road and roams the neighborhood ran up in the yard last week. Normally Flossy would simply have flown over the backyard fence with our other two adult chickens, but now she had babies to protect.

Flossy apparently commanded the peeps to stay put, because they squatted in place and Flossy led the dog away from them and out into the open.

When the dog started after her, she fluffed out her feathers, started making this evil guttural clucking sound, and tried her best to peck out the befuddled dog's eyes.

Jilda saw the altercation, snatched up the BB gun, and put a small piece of copper on the dog's rear end. He immediately understood that the price of a chicken dinner was too high and left the yard in a hurry.

Fast-forward to last Thursday. I was drinking coffee and I heard the chickens sounding the alarm. I've had the birds long enough to recognize the difference between normal clucking and the sound they make when they're frightened.

I walked outside and two of the adult chickens, Bonnie and Clyde, were under the deck. There were no dogs in the back yard, but I caught a glimpse of a hawk out of the corner of my eye.

I ran back inside, got the BB gun, and started firing in the general direction of the hawk to scare it off. Apparently, one shot came close because the predator flew off down toward the barn.

That evening, we noticed that Flossy was missing. The peeps were under the front porch but Flossy was nowhere to be found. She didn't return Friday, either.

I walked to the garden on Saturday and I found her remains. We didn't see what happened, but she must have used the same maneuver with the hawk that she did with the dog.

She ran away from the peeps and out into the open to keep the hawk from killing her babies. She gave her life for theirs.

Jilda and I were both saddened by the loss of our little mama hen, but it made me think about Mother Nature. Flossy's story is not uncommon. History is full of stories of mothers sacrificing their lives for their children.

As I sit on the porch writing this piece, I see the peeps out under the pines scratching for bugs and worms. They live thanks to the bravery and sacrifice of their mom. RIP Flossy.

T·H·I·R·T·Y~S·I·X

War of the Roses

Jilda and I have been engaged in a war in our neighborhood for years. It's not an armed conflict, but a "War of the Roses."

We're in competition with her brother Ricky Phillips to see who has the greenest thumb.

Jilda and I grow great tubs of tomatoes, piles of potatoes, sacks of squash, and pecks of peas. Our apples, pears, blueberries and watermelons are to die for, but our roses look like they've been sprayed with Roundup.

Ricky, on the other hand is a plumber (R&H Plumbing) and doesn't have a lot of time for gardening, but he grows beautiful roses.

We have several bushes, but none of them do very well. The best bush we have is our "John" Rose – our friend John Elliott gave us a cutting many years ago. He has since passed away, but the climbing rose bush he gave us flourishes with roses that are as pink as a baby's cheek. We planted them down at the front of our house on the bank near our mailbox, and we named them after him.

Each year our John bushes throw off thousands of blooms, but they only grow to about the size of a silver dollar. Don't get me wrong, they're beautiful, but they're more like rose-lets. Our other roses are just sad.

Ricky, on the other hand, effortlessly grows roses as big as softballs and bigger. It's a source of contention. He called early this morning to rub a little salt in the wound.

"Hey, one of my pink roses is blooming! Why don't y'all stop by and look at it the next time you're here?" he says over the phone. I can almost hear him snicker. I wanted go over there and smack that smirk off his face, but then who'd bail me out when one of my "simple plumbing repair jobs" goes south and my kitchen is under water? You may recall the recent dishwasher episode. It wasn't pretty.

After Jilda and I finished our walk this morning, we stepped over to his house to have a look. Though it pains me to say it, his roses are stunning. I'm not sure if he puts some kind of special sauce on his bushes, or what, but he spanks us silly each year in the rose war. "I don't do much to them," he says in his Oh-shucks-I'm-just-lucky tone of voice.

I put out a special appeal to my blog buddies across the country asking for help with my roses. A bunch of people responded, but almost everyone was as frustrated as me. My friend Marsha said: I could not even enter, much less win, a race for the roses. But when I stay after the aphids, dig a small trench and only water them from below (the roses, not the aphids), and no more than three times a week, and when I only look at them on the second Tuesday of the fourth week of the month, and if Aquarius is on the rise, and Venus is just above the moon...sometimes, but only sometimes, I can get a wonderful batch for my dining room table.

This was the most encouraging advice I received. Some advice included pruning brutally, adding horse manure, old blood, and egg shells.

I'm still at a loss for how to beat my brother-in-law in the War of the Roses. If you have any helpful advice, please send me an e-mail at cwatson310@charter.net.

T·H·I·R·T·Y~S·E·V·E·N

A Dog Story

My daddy was kind of a horse trader, though he never really owned any horses when we were growing up.

He did wind up with a couple blue tick hounds in a three-way trade that involved whiskey, a rusty pistol, and the hounds.

"Them dogs are the finest coon dogs in the county," the toothless trader said as he took a pull from the bottle of whiskey.

I was about eight years old at the time but I can still remember the old man's eyes kind of glazed over when he took that first sip of moonshine and he scrunched his face up as if he'd hit his thumb with a hammer. When he got his breath back, he managed to rasp, "This ain't bad stuff!"

Everybody shook hands to seal the deal and the dogs hopped into the back of the old pickup truck with me. On the way home, daddy must have experienced "trader's remorse" because he said "I sure hope your mammy don't pitch a hissy fit over them dogs."

The first words out of mama's mouth when we got home were, "I'm not feedin' them dogs, if they get fed, y'all will have to do it."

Daddy looked at me conspiratorially and raised his eyebrows in what looked almost like a flinch, but I recognized it as a signal that said, "Wow, that was easier than I thought!" That night we took the dogs up to Powell Hollow near the old strip pit to see if we could jump a raccoon.

Sure enough, the dogs jumped out of the truck, ran around a few minutes taking care of business, then one of them yelped as if he'd burned his paw, and they were off to the races. Daddy cocked his head and listed to the sound of the dogs, as if he were listening to a symphony orchestra.

We fired up the carbide lanterns and headed after the dogs. It was quiet as a tomb on that crisp autumn night and the sound of their barking made them easy to follow.

All of a sudden we stopped hearing them, which was a little strange. They went from barking every few seconds to not barking at all. It was as if they'd been abducted by alien canine snatchers.

As we walked deeper into the woods, we realized we could hear them, but they sounded far away.

I heard daddy say, "Uh oh, I know what happened." Then he instructed me to stay behind him and walk in his footsteps. It was then I felt a little freaked, as we inched farther into the woods.

Suddenly, the sound of the dogs was getting louder, but there was an echo too.

Then daddy held his hand back and stopped me. He got down on his hands and knees and crawled up to the edge of a mining shaft almost hidden in the brush. When he shined his light down there, he could see the glowing eyes of the dogs about 30 feet down. They were OK, but the hole was too steep for them to climb out.

He then stood up and we headed back to the truck. I asked if we were just going to leave them down there. "We gotta get a rope," he said.

We headed back to the house and he fetched a length of rope and another lamp from the shed.

When we got back to the mining hole, the dogs were still there yapping like crazy. I had wondered on the way back to the hole if Daddy planned to lasso the dogs with the rope or just how the rescue would happen.

It wasn't until he explained that he was going to tie the

rope around my waist and lower me down into the hole to fetch the dogs that my enthusiasm faded.

I was afraid, but I trusted my dad. He gave me the miner's hat with a carbide lamp and he slowly lowered me down.

When I reached the dogs, they licked me like a pork chop. I took the rope from around my waist and tied it to the first dog and daddy slowly pulled him up to safety. We repeated the routine for the second dog, before he dropped the rope back for me.

The entire rescue operation took less than five minutes and I can tell you that even though I was afraid at first, I became the hero of the hour especially to the dogs. My stock also rose with my dad.

I know today, he would probably have been arrested for child endangerment if he pulled a stunt like that, but I was glad I got a chance to shine in the eyes of my dad. And for that, facing a little danger was a small price to pay.

T·H·I·R·T·Y~E·I·G·H·T

Money's Not Everything

I've had a lot of jobs in my life. I've cleaned chicken houses, caught chickens, picked cotton, surveyed on the chain gang with the State Highway Department, and I retired from Ma Bell after 33 years. But I learned more on my first job after I got out of the Army than all the others combined.

Call it fate or serendipity, but my friend Dale Short whom I'd met before I was drafted, was the editor at *The Community News* in Sumiton in 1973 when I returned from active duty.

He called me up to ask if I wanted a job as a writer and photographer. The entry level job didn't pay much, but Uncle Sam had a job retraining program that supplemented my income so that I earned enough to live on, though I probably qualified for food stamps.

What the job lacked in monetary compensation, it made up for with opportunity. For the first time in my life I wasn't doing manual labor, I was using my mental and creative muscles. With Dale as my mentor, I learned to interview people, write stories, shoot pictures, and use a darkroom.

I know that a darkroom is antiquated technology these

days, with the invention of digital cameras, but the darkroom was a great classroom back in the day. There I learned how NOT to shoot a picture.

These days if you take a bad picture, you simply delete it and shoot another. That didn't work with a film camera. When you shot a bad picture you'd often spend hours in the darkroom trying to print something decent for publication--and in those days, Mr. Short was a taskmaster!

"Yeah, this would look pretty good," he'd say, "if the kid didn't have a tree-limb growing out of his ear".

So I'd skulk back to the darkroom to use dodging and burning techniques to try and remove the limb. I learned that you should ALWAYS check the background to make sure it doesn't make the person in the picture look goofy. Unless of course you didn't like the person and you wanted to make them look goofy.

The Community News weekly often looked like a magazine. We didn't do hard news, but features, interviews, and eye-popping photo layouts that spanned two full pages.

Dale had worked as a writer for an over-the-mountain newspaper in Birmingham before coming to *The Community News*, but was fired because the publisher said, "Dale, you just can't write."

In 1974 we entered *The Community News* in the Alabama Press Association's Better Newspaper contest, and we all got a free weekend down at the State Convention Center in Gulf Shores to attend the awards event.

It was serendipity at work again, because our seats were directly across from the publisher who'd fired Dale.

We racked up that night, as *The Community News* took first-place honors in many of the major categories including Best Weekly Newspaper, Best Editorial, Best Use of Photography, Best Feature Article, and Best Looking Staff. (OK, I made that one up, but we did look pretty snazzy hauling all those awards back to the table.)

In all, the paper won 11 awards--which at that time was the most awards any weekly newspaper had ever won at one event. The publisher who'd fired Dale won a single award. As I recall it was for eating the most crow.

The three years I spent at *The Community News* were a gift. It was one of the most rewarding jobs I've ever had. Even though the job didn't pay that well, the things I took away from it proved to be invaluable throughout my life.

It was there I learned that work is not always about the money. Sometimes you learn things that are more valuable that a paycheck.

T·H·I·R·T·Y~N·I·N·E

Some Things Are Scarier Than Snakes

I found out last week there that are things much scarier than snakes, spiders and drug-addled drivers on the wrong side of the road.

What scared the living daylights out of me was an irregular shaped spot the size of a pencil eraser that appeared on Jilda's forearm just above her left wrist.

Jilda has blonde hair, blue eyes and skin that's as white as Casper the friendly ghost. She is super mindful about the sun – I think she wears sun block to bed at night, but even with all the caution, a place came up on her face last year.

She went to one doctor at UAB who looked at the tiny place on her nose and said it was nothing to be concerned with. Jilda had a feeling that didn't sit well, so she got a second opinion and as it turns out, the tiny spot was basal cell carcinoma. It had to go.

The doctor did a remarkable job with the surgery, leaving only a tiny scar that only she can see.

His instructions to her were very clear - if ANYTHING comes up that looks odd, come see me immediately. "Tell the receptionist you need an appointment now."

Ever since then, I routinely check her like I'm looking for ticks. She was out of town for yoga training when the place appeared and she showed it to me when she got home on Sunday. I wanted to call the doctor right then, but she convinced me to wait until the morning.

That Sunday night was a very long night for me. I slept fitfully and each time I woke up, I laid awake wondering what on earth I would do if something happened to her.

We started dating on my graduation night in May of 1968. We broke up for a while during my stint in the Army but we were thick as thieves when my tour was over and we tied the knot in 1974.

Some married couples practically live separate lives, having different hobbies, interests and world views. That's not the case with us.

We've always enjoyed a lot of the same things. We love writing and playing music, traveling, gardening, and entertaining friends.

I always thought culture was what grew on cheese when it stayed in your fridge too long, but she's taught me through the years about the finer things in life that would have slipped right by me.

She's one of the most creative people I know and she's downright funny. Heck, I wouldn't have anything to write about if it weren't for her.

I went to the doctor with her on Tuesday. To say that I was wound up tight as a piano wire as we waited to be called back to see the dermatologist is an understatement.

When the doctor told her the small place was a type of bruise and nothing to worry about, I was so relieved, I almost wet my pants.

I'm not a pray-er by nature. I figure the Good Lord has a lot more important things to worry about than most of my petty grievances. I save my requests for my closest friends and family members when they are hurting, sick, or in need.

I did say a prayer on Tuesday, and I made a promise to never take my wife for granted again. It is my intention to keep that promise.

F•O•R•T•Y

Encyclopedia

I was curious about something today so I whipped out my iPhone, touched the Wikipedia icon, and had the answer within a matter of seconds.

That experience sent my mind ambling down a path it had not been down in years -- my family's first set of encyclopedias.

I learned to spell encyclopedia at a fairly early age. I didn't watch a lot of TV but I did watch Jiminy Cricket on Disney. I can still recall the little tune he sang ENCY---CLO--PEDIA.

In the early 1960's a salesman knocked on our door in West Pratt. He was selling World Book Encyclopedias.

Not many salesmen got to the front porch, much less got a chance to sit in our living room and drink a glass of sweet tea. But this one did.

He gave his spiel, and the words he used must have resonated with my mom, because he got a chance to get to second base -- actually showing us the books.

The salesman laid a cloth on our kitchen table, and handled the books as if they were fine crystal. He laid a few out so we could get a better look. They were bound in red leather, and the edges of the pages were trimmed in gold.

My mother was frugal, to the point of squeezing her dollars so tightly that George Washington thought he had asthma.

The kids left the kitchen so that mama could talk to the salesman about the price. I don't remember how much they were, but even then, they were very expensive. I was nine and my older brother and sister were in high school.

I know my mom thought long and hard about what it would take to pay for the books, but all three of us were in school at the time, and education was VERY important to her.

Apparently the salesman knocked the ball out of the park, because she agreed to buy the books.

She paid them off in installments with money she made washing and ironing clothes for people around Dora.

My dad had a job, but it took all the money he made to keep us fed, so mama paid for most of the extras by doing laundry.

A few days later the salesman delivered the books. I can remember sitting on the kitchen table poring through the pages; traveling to places I had never imagined. London, Prague, and Minnesota.

I also learned about other things too. Aardvarks. Who knew there was an animal with such a strange name?

The pages were thin as a whisper and they smelled....... of knowledge. In a way, those books were like the World Wide Web without the porn.

A few years ago when we had to sell my mom's house, I went through looking for the World Book Encyclopedias, but I couldn't find them.

I'm guessing she gave them to someone who had kids that might need them. I'd like to think that whoever wound up with the books got a chance to travel to places they'd never imagined.

F·O·R·T·Y~O·N·E

A Drive Down Memory Lane

Jilda worked yesterday and I was supposed to be writing this column. But sometimes, no matter how hard I try, the words won't come.

I decided to go for a drive. Sometimes driving with no set destination opens pathways in my mind and allows me to think.

Yesterday I drove down through Sloss Hollow and by the place where I spent most of my childhood.

There's not much there anymore. When the new road came through in 1969 (I'm not sure why I still call it the new road), it changed the landscape of my community forever. The state bought all the houses on the west side of the road, and demolished most of them. My friends scattered like startled quail.

When I glanced in my rearview mirror, there were several cars behind me, and I realized I was driving 15 mph below the speed limit,. I hit my blinker and I pulled off to let them pass.

I got some nasty looks as they wheeled around me, but

I'd like to think they would have cut me some slack had they known I was driving down memory lane.

Since it was 93 degrees, I left my truck idling so I wouldn't roast like a Walmart chicken.

As I looked around me, I realized that a great deal of my young life was spent within a hundred yards of where I was sitting.

Sitting on my daddy's lap, I learned to steer a car right here on the old tar and gravel road that ran in front of our house. I also learned to ride a bicycle here with my sister Mary Lois running beside me to keep me stable until I found my balance.

Traffic was infrequent, so we also played baseball on that road; it's where I learned to throw a curve ball.

This place is also where I learned to tend chickens, and grow tomatoes; where I learned to shoot a gun, and fish. It's where I experienced the first true fear of my life when I walked up on a cottonmouth moccasin on the bank of the creek that ran through the community.

The Parkers lived across the road from us, and they had kinfolk from up north who visited each year. One summer cousins Joe and Alan came to visit the Parker kids, Edward,

Tommy and Susie. Joe brought his guitar.

It was there, sitting on their front-porch swing that I strummed my first awkward chord on a guitar. It sounded almost as bad as fingernails on a chalkboard, but my love of playing music began on that sweltering August evening and it's remained with me all my life.

Once when an old freight train rattled down the track that dissected West Pratt, I discovered that you could make a penny as big around as a quarter and thin as a postage stamp by placing it on a rail.

As I sat there yesterday replaying the old tapes in my head, I took out a notebook and smiled as I jotted down notes.

There's nothing like strolling down memory lane to get the creative juices flowing.

F·O·R·T·Y~T·W·O

Tattoos

The first tattoo I ever saw was of a naked woman on my grandpa Charlie Watson's forearm. I'm sure the figure was racy when he got it, but the years had erased most of the tattoo. What remained looked as if it had been sketched with a blue ballpoint pen.

The figure went from his wrist to his elbow and I always wondered about the story behind that tattoo. I'd be willing to bet Mama Watson hit the roof when he came home with it, but I never asked.

Back in the day, tattoos were mostly found on the arms of sailors, bikers, and people who'd spent time in jail. But to my knowledge my grandpa was never in the Navy, rode a Harley, or did any time "bustin' rocks" on a chain-gang.

According to the *Smithsonian Magazine*, humans have marked their bodies with tattoos for thousands of years. These permanent designs—sometimes plain, sometimes elaborate, always personal—have served as amulets, status symbols, declarations of love, signs of religious beliefs, adornments, and even forms of punishment.

These days, tattoos are common on both men and

women. I was standing in the checkout line at Walmart this past week people-watching. I'm fascinated by what people wear to Walmart, and what they have in their buggies.

Anyhow, I noticed a woman in front of me who was wearing a fairly short skirt. A splash of color on her leg drew my eyes down just below her hemline. Turns out she had a beautiful rose tattoo on the back of her thigh just above the knee.

She must have sensed me staring and turned around. I snapped my head away so quickly I almost got whiplash, and my face turned the color of a ripe tomato.

I busied myself surveying the contents of my buggy and eventually the blood returned to the rest of my body. I'm sure her tattoo had a story but I was too embarrassed to ask.

I have a tattoo that I got in 1972 when I was stationed in Panama during my stint in the Army.

It was a holiday weekend and a bunch of us guys were all sitting around the barracks knocking back a few brews when someone said, "Hey, I've got a great idea -- let's all go get tattoos!"

That sounded like a splendid idea, so we caught a bus and headed off in search of a tattoo parlor.

We ventured into an area that was the underbelly of the city and always smelled of fish and diesel fuel.

We found a place that was a little ratty, but the lights were on and the tattoo pictures in the window were colorful, so we went inside to get the scoop.

The female tattoo artist was about 30 and couldn't speak a word of English. That was unfortunate because none of us could speak Spanish. We quickly figured out that talking louder didn't get the message across, so the deal went down using sign language.

Looking through the tattoo book I saw tons of designs, but they cost more than I could afford so I pointed to a small butterfly.

No one was keen on going first, so I volunteered. I've heard people say that getting tattoos doesn't hurt, but they lied.

Mine felt like she was using a handheld Singer sewing machine with a dull needle. The liquid courage had worn off before she completed the first wing. As she laid down the design, I actually think my skin smoked.

All the guys gathered around and watched and my friend Doug took pictures. I'm not sure if it was the skin smoke, or the guttural moans I was making, but for some reason everyone else decided that tattoos weren't for them.

I was the only one who went home with permanent artwork on my shoulder. And that's the story behind my tattoo.

Like my grandpa, time has taken all but the faintest outline of the butterfly on my right shoulder blade. But I bet his story was a lot more interesting than mine.

F•O•R•T•Y~T•H•R•E•E

Terror Girl

I had no clue that my wife Jilda was a terrorist. Yes, she got crossways with the Department of Homeland Security when we traveled to Los Angeles for a songwriter conference a few years ago.

The groundwork for the evil plan was laid at birth. Some say the plot was hatched by a local doctor, and others say it was the handiwork of her mom who was cranked up on birthing drugs. Instead of J-I-L-D-A, her "permanent record" wound up G-I-L-D-A.

She's always gone by Jilda, which never caused a problem until 9/11. Now, every time we board an aircraft she gets hassled. That November we managed to fly out of Birmingham without getting Maced, but the return trip was a different story.

We arrived at the LA airport at 4 a.m. and the pre-security screener caught the discrepancy between "Gilda" on her photo ID and "Jilda" on her airline boarding pass. She immediately jabbed a big honkin' RED STAMP on the boarding pass and said "they can help you at the next security checkpoint."

As we approached the checkpoint, they sent me down the normal line and they sent Jilda down the terrorist line. She was in this glass tunnel-like enclosure along with a guy who looked Persian, another guy that looked like one of those weird Japanese cult members, and a Middle-Eastern woman who was menacing the hired help. "You are singling us out," she hissed in broken English – PROFILING!!!!

I could not hear everything from my vantage point outside the Terror-Aquarium, but Jilda was looking around at the Middle-Easterner as if to say, what is this "we" stuff, lady? I'm from Empire, Alabama and the closest thing to terrorism I've ever done was to push over an outhouse when I was 16 years old! I could almost hear the Middle Eastern woman saying "Save it for the judge, GILDA!"

I thought things were about to get ugly when the lady security officer started snapping on rubber gloves. I can think of few occasions involving rubber gloves that turned out well.

I guess Jilda thought I was going to bail out on her to save my own skin. She was hollering through the glass, trying to tell me not to leave her to the wolves. The rubber-gloved screener whacked the glass with a stick and told Jilda to look straight ahead.

There was a very nice senior screener guy (he'd been a screener longer than three months) standing there with me and

I asked if they were going to do a strip search on my wife. He grinned and said that they had to do a really thorough search whenever there is any kind of discrepancy in the traveler's documentation.

After that, the situation became much lighter for me but unfortunately Jilda could not hear those soothing words and she was still freaked. They searched her purse, her shoes, checked her for explosives, and did the magic wand to check for firearms. When they set her free, she was visibly shaken and when she saw me laughing she was one angry wife. I was so close to the doghouse I could smell the Kibbles and Bits.

Things went smoothly after that, and it's actually comforting to know that these security folks are taking their job very seriously. As we boarded the plane for home, I poked her in the ribs and said "Look on the bright side, you're now probably on the Department of Homeland Security's Terrorist Watch List."

That trip was the straw that broke the camel's back, because she vowed to get the spelling of the name on her birth certificate corrected. This week she finally set the record straight with the Department of Homeland Security when she received the corrected documents.

I think we can all rest better now.

F·O·R·T·Y~F·O·U·R

Twenty Five Years

I pulled *To Kill a Mockingbird* from our library shelf today and something slipped from between pages. When I picked it up, I realized that it was the laminated obituary for my dad who died in the spring of 1986.

It's hard to believe that it's been almost 25 years since we lost him. I reflexively wiped my thumb across the picture, and stepped closer to the light filtering through the window to get a better look. As I read the obit again, it occurred to me that I am now just two years younger than he was when he passed away. A wave of sadness came over me and I fought back tears.

Back in 1986, I remember thinking how old he looked just before he died. The last few years of his life had not been kind to him, and he seemed to look more tired and frail each time we visited.

He worked hard as a welder for most of his life, and he spent every free moment in the woods or on the river. He loved the outdoors.

After he got sick and couldn't drive, he spent most of his time sitting in a recliner in the corner of the living room. I think toward the end he'd made up his mind he was ready to go.

I was in Atlanta on business when my mom phoned my office to tell me he'd been rushed to the hospital. They tracked me down in Atlanta to give me the message. My boss at the time wanted me to stay for a meeting but I told him I felt like I needed to go home.

He wasn't happy, but I really didn't leave room for negotiation. When I landed in Birmingham, Jilda picked me up at the airport and whisked me to the hospital.

I went straight to intensive care to see him and he gave me a faint smile when I took his hand.

I hadn't been there 20 minutes before the machines began to beep slower and his vital signs weakened. With my brother Neil and me holding his hands, he slipped away.

Even though it's been 25 years since my father died, I can still smell the aroma of his Rose Hair Oil, and remember the short black comb he carried in his right hip pocket next to his wallet. I can hear the clattering sound his keys made when he laid them on the dresser next to his bed at night.

He had an Army footlocker as old as the hills that he'd painted white with a brush. It's where he kept his personal things.

After he died, mama wanted me to go through the trunk and try to figure out what to do with what he had left behind.

Inside the trunk was a lifetime of souvenirs. An Old Timer pocket knife, an ink pen with the image of a woman in a bathing suit. When you turned the pen upside down, the bathing suit disappeared. He also had some cat-eye marbles, and an antique Zippo lighter with the cover worn smooth on one side from years of flipping and zipping.

It was an interesting experience browsing through the things that my father had kept for all those years.

A ringing phone snatched me back to the present, and as I cradled the phone between my shoulder and ear, I put daddy's obit back between the pages of *To Kill a Mockingbird*. I know it will make me sad again the next time I run across it, but the bookmark will also help me to hold onto memories of my dad.

F·O·R·T·Y~F·I·V·E

Valentine's Day

Today is Valentine's Day. And guys, if you haven't already gotten your honey something sweet, you still have some time. One word of advice -- be mindful of what you get.

As I've written before, I've bought some unfortunate gifts for my spouse on Valentine's Day so I feel qualified to speak on the topic, and indeed obligated to my peeps to share what I've learned through the years. There are commercials a-plenty to tell you what to buy. My mission today is to tell you what NOT to buy.

An umbrella is one of the handiest tools ever invented. It's the first thing I reach for on rainy days, but I'm here to tell you that they are unsuitable as Valentine's gifts. I don't care if it's red and smells like roses, STEP AWAY FROM THE UMBRELLA!

I had a friend who got this wacky idea to give his wife some bricks as a gift. It was his way of telling his lovely bride that he was building a new house for her. After years of living in a rental that was a dump, he thought the bricks on Valentine's Day would be symbolic. He believed in his heart that this gesture was perfect, and that she'd be moved to tears.

But no. In fact she came up with some new creative uses of bricks that he had never heard of before. Had he followed through with her instructions of where he could put the bricks, it would have made sitting very uncomfortable for him. He stayed in the doghouse so long he started to enjoy the taste of Milk Bones.

I've also learned in my 35 years of marriage that kitchen utensils can be problematic gifts on anniversaries or Valentine's Day, so don't fall into THAT trap.

Other gifts you may want to steer clear of are exercise DVDs, gym memberships, or workout clothes. You may think it's a practical gift, but to a woman it screams "You're fat!" This can send you down a slippery path, my friend, and you could wind up so bruised that your mama won't recognize you. Years of valuable experience at work here. Listen to what I say. STEP AWAY FROM THE WEIGHT LOSS SECTION OF THE STORE!!!

Here's another shocker for men. Most women don't want lingerie for Valentine's Day. I know that some of you guys out there think I'm out of my mind, but it's true -- not that I'm out of my mind, but that most women don't want underwear for V-Day.

You may think the gift is for her, but women understand

the gift is REALLY for you. It took me years and truckloads of frozen TV dinners to figure this out. You get this info free just by being a subscriber to *The Daily Mountain Eagle*.

A good Valentine's Day gift doesn't have to cost a lot of money. I made a gift for Jilda one year when we were strapped for cash. It was a coupon book and the coupons were good for a free car wash, a free meal at Rick's Diner (she never actually cashed this one in, possibly because I can't cook), a back massage, and other favors that would be imprudent to discuss in a family paper. The point is, it didn't cost anything except a little thought and some creativity.

Of course, you could always spring for the ultimate Valentine's Day gift, which is a copy of my book *Remembering Big*, available at fine gift shops, restaurants, and other establishments around the area.

I know, I know, it's shameless self promotion. But the cover is red, and if I can sell a few copies maybe I can take Jilda out for dinner tonight.

Happy Valentine's Day.

F·O·R·T·Y~S·I·X

Water Bill

My water bill was through the roof last month. I called the Jasper Water Works and told them my bill had almost doubled. I was not happy and I wanted to share that with someone.

I told the lady who answered the phone that I needed someone to yell at. I guess she could tell by the tone of my voice that even though I was concerned about my bill, I wasn't really the yelling kind, so she volunteered to take the tongue-lashing.

She listened intently, and after a few minutes she told me they have new-fangled meters these days and that she could get to the bottom of the situation.

The lady said the meter indeed showed I WAS using a lot of water, almost twice as much as normal.

I had a sinking feeling that I might have a water leak, which was unfortunate for me because it took the monkey off their backs and put it squarely on mine. The investigation began.

My pipes have been spliced a few times during the 30

years we've lived here, so I knew pretty much where to look. The last issue we had was under the deck, so that's where I started. After 20 minutes of digging, I unearthed the pipe and it was not leaking.

The second place was out by the apple tree where the old standpipe once stood. The moment I stepped on the sharpshooter shovel, it sank to the hilt. I was so glad that I hadn't really been ugly to the lady at the water works, cause I would have been eating some crow.

I turned the water off and had started to repair the leak when I realized I needed a new fitting. I keep all kinds of stuff in my tool shed, but after turning it upside down I realized I didn't have the right one.

I went to plan B, which is to look in the barn and in Sharky's old truck.

Sharky was Jilda's dad and he was a plumber from way back. In addition to doing plumbing work, he was a pack rat who never threw anything away. Through the years, that's been a blessing for me, because whenever I need a tool or some other obscure part, I can usually find it in the barn.

Sharky had bins, buckets, and shelves where he stored nuts, bolts, screws, and fittings. More often than not, I can find what I'm looking for somewhere in there.

Unfortunately I didn't find it in the barn this time, so I decided to look in his old blue Ford pickup, parked behind the barn.

I opened the door, scooted in the passenger side, and started going through the boxes and sacks in the floorboard of the old workhorse. I moved a plastic garbage bag from the driver's side of the seat and uncovered a snake coiled up that looked as big as Rhode Island.

You could say I exited the truck quickly, but that would not have captured the level of haste I used to get out of that pickup. I bumped my head, my knee, and both elbows. I didn't mess my britches, but I came close. I let out a stream of cuss words that would have gotten me "whupped with a rosebush" if my mama had heard it.

Now, I'm not sure if it was a rattlesnake or just an old chicken snake, because I didn't hang around long enough to make the proper identification. I realized in billionths of a second that I'd seen as much of the cab of that truck as I needed to see. I left a pair of pliers in the cab of Old Blue, but I think I'll leave them there until maybe December when snakes hibernate.

I went to the hardware store and bought a fitting to fix my water leak, so hopefully I won't have to pawn my truck to pay next month's water bill.

If anyone wants a great deal on an old Ford pickup, just let me know. I'll throw the snake in, free.

F·O·R·T·Y~S·E·V·E·N

Sunsets

It's been as cold as a well digger's…..well, let's just say it's been really cold and dreary lately. I can take a day or two without sunshine, but too many dark days give me a case of the blues. When the sun finally made an appearance, my spirits lifted.

On the way home from my day gig, I got to catch my first sunset in months. I was on Arkadelphia Road near the border of Walker and Blount counties at the ridge of a mountain (it's really just a foothill, but here in Alabama, we call them mountains).

At the crest of the mountain, it looks as though you can see across Walker County and all the way to Mississippi.

The sun glowed like an amber egg sinking down toward the horizon. The scene was so breathtaking I pulled over to the side of the road to enjoy the waning moments of the descent. As I watched, the western sky turned the color of a rusty garden plow.

I snapped a few frames. No camera can capture the magnificence of a sunset, but I always try.

In looking back through the thousands of photographs I've taken in my life, one would discover that a good many of my photographs are dedicated to sunsets.

Some of my earliest sunset photos are from Panama where I bought my first real camera, but the portfolio has grown steadily since the early Seventies.

Several years ago, we took our niece Samantha to San Francisco and one evening we drove south of the city to Santa Cruz and walked down the boardwalk at sunset. We bought ice cream cones and strolled along soaking in the atmosphere. We stopped for a while, dangled our legs off the edge of the weathered pier, and paid a silent tribute to a sunset that was indescribably beautiful.

I've never been to Hawaii but friends have told me that sunsets there are something to behold. I'd really like to go and see for myself. One of our main goals when we visited Ireland was to watch a sunset off the west coast of the Arian Islands, and we scheduled that treat a few days before departure.

When we went to board the ferry, they told us that fog sometimes makes a day trip turn into a several-day trip, so we had to scratch that off our list.

Even when things are chaotic and my life seems like it's spiraling out of control, a sunset will stop me in my tracks and give me a chance to put my priorities in order.

Life has a way of filling up any unallocated time. If you don't take some time for yourself, someone else will take it and make it their own.

I'm not sure about you, but I'm getting too old to let that happen. There's more sand at the bottom of my hourglass than at the top and what's left is precious to me.

Mother Nature provides an unending slide show; from an unfathomable night sky in summer, to autumn leaves, or a blanket of fresh snow in winter.

I can't imagine a better cure for the blues than a January sunset.

F•O•R•T•Y~E•I•G•H•T

Knee Therapy

My daddy used to have a saying about people who are lucky – "Why, he could step in a bucket of cow manure and he'd come out smelling like a rose."

While I always thought it was strange that someone would have a bucket of cow manure, the lesson was not lost on me, and this week I felt like the guy who did the stepping.

My knees have been giving me fits for the last few months. When I get up in the morning, they squeak and click. I've seen a few doctors, one of which shot my knees full of some kind of medicine, using a needle that looked as big as a kindergarten pencil. I'm here to tell you that was not fun.

Another doctor prescribed some medication that fights inflammation, and it did seem to help for a few days, but that old familiar pain returned. It still felt like a toothache, except it was in my knees.

Jilda, who is AAD (almost a doctor) has been telling me for months to try acupuncture. I've used acupuncture before when my back was giving me fits, and it did help. Now that I think of it, I haven't had a problem with my back since then.

I decided to go to the local chiropractor/acupuncture specialist and finally I've found a specialist who understands the problem and has prescribed therapy that's just right for my condition.

After a session of acupuncture and electric stimulation therapy, my knees did feel better.

As I settled up at the front desk, the doctor instructed me to apply cold compresses to my knees.

Just then, an idea flashed in my brain as bright as a lightning strike. This news was too good to be true. Bear with me, because this gets complicated.

I reasoned that the water flowing out from Smith Dam where I fly fish is 52 degrees and colder most of the year.

When you fly fish, you wade out waist deep in the frigid water, so as it turns out, my doctor prescribed fly fishing for my ailing knees. Well not really, but even a simpleton could make this connection – the icy waters of the Sipsey Fork of the Black Warrior River is at least as good for my knees as a cold compress. I could have hugged her neck. It was almost like hitting the lottery!

Now Jilda is one of the kindest, most caring people on the planet but I feared I might be "dancin' with the devil" trying to slide this idea by her.

So I did some rehearsing – "Yes dear, I'd love to cut the grass, and weed the garden, but it's time for my cold therapy."

Turns out, she wasn't a hard sell at all, so the next morning I went for knee therapy. It's tough, but I'm willing to go the extra mile to get my health back.

I figure by the end of the year, I should have knees like a 20-year old. Is this a great country or what?

Honey, I'm going fishing today -- doctor's orders.

F•O•R•T•Y~N•I•N•E

There's Power In Words

There's power in words. I've said that time and again, but last night as I struggled to think of a topic for this column I picked up a journal from 1992 and read an entry I wrote long before I became a freelance writer.

I wrote -- "I want to take pictures, play music, and write stories about interesting people."

At the time, I was a night shift supervisor for the phone company in a data center, and at times I felt like a ship lost at sea without engine, compass, or rudder. It was a good job, but I longed to do more with my life.

I was trapped by the security of my job. We needed insurance, we had bills to pay, so we had to have a steady paycheck.

We'd built a new house a few years before, and I wanted to go back to college for my Master's degree, but I felt that was a pipe dream without a steady job with a regular paycheck.

It seemed crazy at the time to even consider doing anything else, but that didn't stop me from writing those words in my journal.

I laughed out loud as I read that passage tonight. Because today, I shot photographs of high school kids who'd received sports scholarships to colleges around the country.

This afternoon, I interviewed a man who played football on a University of Alabama football team that won two national championships. He got a great job after college, got married, had kids, then lost it all when he got strung out on pain meds after problems with kidney stones.

He was homeless for a few years -- he pawned his college national championship rings to buy drugs.

I don't want to say too much right now, because the story has not been published, but he did turn his life around and his story is nothing less than remarkable. I'd say he was an interesting person to interview.

Tonight, Jilda and I are finalizing our set list for our gig tomorrow night. In the past year, we've played at festivals, art galleries, and coffee houses around the area. We don't make a great deal of money, but playing music seems to be good for the soul.

So maybe you can see why I smiled when I read the entry from 1992 -- I want to take pictures, play music, and write stories about interesting people.

I think everybody has dreams, but I guess too many believe their dreams could never come true. Back in 1992, I didn't know how I would ever make my words come to life, but those dreams were important enough to me that I wrote them down in my journal.

Things didn't happen overnight, but I marched steadily in the direction of my dreams.

I think I can say with some authority that words have power. Even if you don't see any way possible that you can make something happen in your life, write down what you want.

I'm living proof that it pays off.

F·I·F·T·Y

Blackie Bear

There's an old saying that says (I'm paraphrasing): "You're stuck with your family, but you can choose your friends." The same is true for dogs.

Blackie Bear, a black lab with enough chow mixed in to make his tongue spotted, came to live with us back in 1997.

Our niece Samantha, who was in kindergarten at the time, found him wandering around Sumiton School and she somehow convinced her mom to bring the dog home.

He was still a puppy then, and it was obvious he'd been abandoned because he was as thin as a hobo's dog. He had paws almost as big as my hand so I knew he would become a big dog with some nourishment.

She told us, when she brought him over to show him off, that he was looking for a home. We wrongly assumed that home would be at Samantha's house, but as it turns out, he never left our house, because he'd found his home. We had several older dogs at the time but Blackie was a kind and gentle spirit and found his place in the pack.

He was a bit of a loner and whenever we walked, he

would never walk on the trail with us. He preferred walking through the thickest brambles and briar patches he could find.

He would disappear for hours only to return in the evening covered in mud and pond scum. I spent many afternoons hosing him down in the back yard while he grunted and groaned with obvious pleasure.

He loved swimming in the strip pits, ponds and creeks behind the barn. He did this even in the dead of winter. One afternoon in January when the mercury was in the twenties, he ambled up from his swimming excursion with ice crystals on his coat.

As the older dogs passed on, Blackie moved up in the family hierarchy until he became Jilda's number one dog. He took that role seriously. When she walked, he walked. When she fixed dinner, he lay on the cool tile in the middle of the kitchen floor supervising. This part of his guard duty paid huge dividends because she often "accidentally" dropped a piece of cheese, or a small piece of chicken.

A few years ago his health began to fail. His joints stiffened and his heart grew weak, but he was a trooper. The heat this summer took its toll on him and he found it harder to breathe when he went outside to walk with us.

This year when Jilda began treatments for her immune

system issue, he remained faithfully by her side. When one of the other dogs came near her to be petted, Blackie stood between them and did his low growl which let the other dogs know to keep away.

This week, Jilda ran out of steam and decided to lie down on the couch to rest for a while. Blackie came up and nudged her hand. Jilda petted and hugged him and he walked off.

A short time later, our other dogs began acting strangely and Jilda got up to investigate. I was on the screened porch writing when I heard her calling for Blackie. I could hear concern in her voice so I went out too.

We walked to the barn and back through the hollow. We searched the front and back yards. Jilda's voice turned from concern, to panic, to a pleading sadness that broke my heart. I walked out to the edge of the back yard where we pile brush to burn every now and then, and when I walked to the back side, Blackie had crawled under some of the brush and died. He was still warm when I found him. We both cried as if we'd lost a child.

I dug his grave with a pick and shovel and laid him to rest in a place of honor, next to our other dogs. I placed a peace stone I'd made at the head of his grave.

Our house has been a melancholy place this week. I know there are people who might say we are silly to weep over a dog, but I don't know of anyone who could have had a better friend. I am thankful he chose our home all those years ago.